# Confessions of a Streetwalker

# Confessions

## of a **Streetwalker**

Molly, Me, and Jan Make Three

David L. McKenna

RESOURCE *Publications* · Eugene, Oregon

CONFESSIONS OF A STREETWALKER
Molly, Me, and Jan Makes Three

Resource Publications
An Imprint of Wipf and Stock Publishers
199 W. 8th Ave., Suite 3
Eugene, OR 97401

www.wipfandstock.com

PAPERBACK ISBN: 978-1-4982-8949-8
HARDCOVER ISBN: 978-1-4982-8951-1

Manufactured in the U.S.A.

Dedicated to:

Plain People
who
Walk Daily
and
Serve Joyfully
in
Common Places

# Contents

# Introduction

# "Just Plain Dave"

*"Organizational charts and fancy titles
count next to nothing."*

—Colin Powell[1]

I am spoiled. In a career in higher education that spanned more than 50 years I had the advantage of: prestigious titles, both earned and honorary; strong institutions of higher education, both private and public; and supportive cultures, both church and community. Although I do not believe that I let these entitlements define me as a person, I would be foolish to deny that they had no significant influence on my self-image and on the expectations of those who knew me. As I look back upon these advantages, I realize how they can become driving forces on which we depend.

## Identity by Title

In one of my relaxing "do-nothing" moments of retirement, I thought back over a career that began in 1950 and jotted down the titles by which I have been known over the next 65 years – Reverend, Dean, Doctor, Professor, President, President Emeritus, Trustee, Chair of the Board, Chair Emeritus, and Founding Chair. You can imagine how spoiled I became with all of these titles attached to my name, especially when I was addressed as "President McKenna" or "Dr. McKenna."

During the days of campus protest in the early 1970s, a student rebel barged into my office and demanded to see "Dave." My Executive Assistant, Cec Tindall, gave him a steely, withering eye and said, "You may have an appointment with President McKenna, but Dave is not available." He got the message. When he came into the office, he sheepishly addressed me as "President McKenna." Such protection adds to the spoiling process. For 65 years, only my immediate family, long-time friends, and close colleagues called me "Dave."

# Affiliation by Institution

Add to this list of titles the names of the institutions where I served in sequence—Spring Arbor College (now University), Seattle Pacific College (now University) and Asbury Theological Seminary. Fred Smith, my mentor, reminded me that as president, I was the "face" of the institution. In each of the institutions where I served I was entrusted with its long-term history, its succession in leadership, and its credibility in higher education. Yet, I dared not make the fatal mistake of assuming that the deference of being president belonged to me rather than to the office. President Harry S. Truman once said something like this, "If I ever think that the band is playing 'Hail to the Chief' in honor of me rather than the office that I hold, we are all in trouble."[2] His warning emphasizes the fact that individuals are elevated by the institutions they represent. At best, we are stewards, not owners, of the offices we hold and the titles we carry.

Still, we count on the reputation of the institution to give us credibility. It is a bit like the maxim for selecting a book to read: "If you don't know the author, know the publisher." So, whenever I introduced myself as "President" I quickly added the name of the institution that bolstered my standing. It worked until I served on educational boards or committees with presidents from Ivy League schools. Just the name "Harvard, Yale, or Princeton" made everyone stand up, take notice, and pay attention to the person who carried the title "President." When my turn came to introduce myself and the institution I represented, blank looks revealed the unspoken questions, "Where's that?" and "What are you doing here?" More than once, in that competitive company, I confess that I went past my institutional identity with a Christian college or university and quickly added my stints on the faculty of the University of Michigan and The Ohio State University. Shame on me. But don't we all do the same?

## Assurance by Culture

Throughout my career I also had the benefit of support from a local church culture and a church-related constituency. Spring Arbor University is located in a mid-western town of a couple thousand people; Seattle Pacific University is a conclave of school and church surrounded by urban diversity; and Asbury Theological Seminary, along with Asbury University, dominates the population of a Kentucky village on the edge of Appalachia. In these settings, the president is dearly loved at the same time that the subtleties of social pressure set up limits on behavior, feed the grapevine, and raise the expectations for performance. Long before the advent of social media, the interpersonal networks of these communities could make or break a president. The same was true for the "hidden power" of informal networks in the institutions where I served. Early on, I learned about the power of the faculty coffee table and the leverage of the senior member who presided at the sessions. With a bit fiendish glee, I periodically appeared at the table just to watch the faces droop and the conversation lag. On balance, however, the holder of presidential office in these settings can count on the culture for moral support and spiritual strength.

## "Dave Who?"

What if all these advantages were cancelled in the blink of an eye? Imagine losing our identification by title, affiliation by institution, and assurance by culture all at once. This happened to me in 2005 when Jan and I moved into a down-sized and up-priced condo in Kirkland, Washington along the shores of Lake Washington. Although Kirkland still has the character of a resort village along the Lake, it is surrounded by the burgeoning metropolis of Seattle. Overnight, Jan and I became residents in an urban world known for its anonymity, diversity, and secular mindset. For the first time in 50 years I found myself without an honorific title, an affiliated institution, or the assurance of a church-related culture. Even more disarming, I walked into a world "where nobody knows my name." On my daily walks along Lake Street and through the village of Kirkland, I joined the company of streetwalkers who remain anonymous behind double dark sunglasses, hooded jackets, and ubiquitous headphones.

When I first began walking the streets of Kirkland, I complained, "How can this be? Doesn't anyone remember that I was President of Seattle Pacific University for 14 years? Aren't there any alumni walking these streets who might recognize me as 'Dr. McKenna'?" Alas, my deflated sense of self-esteem continued to take its hits. One day a man on the street asked me if I had a business card. While active in my career, I never left home without business cards in my billfold and when someone asked for one, I was the fastest draw in the West or wherever I found myself. But now, for the first time in more than 50 years, I was unarmed. Even though boxes of business cards engraved with past titles were still in the storage room, none of them was relevant to my status as a retiree walking the streets. So, I had to answer, "Sorry, I have no business card." The look I got matched the look at someone who had just confessed that he was less than human. I was "title-less" – a non-entity to be pitied.

Alpha dogs always take charge of such situations. I went online to check out bargain prices on boxes of business cards. After finding a sophisticated design for a card I confronted the blank space asking for "Title." What would I call myself? Several options came to mind. I could legitimately claim the title of "President Emeritus" or "President (Retired)" of three institutions. Or I could promote my retirement standing as an "Author" or "Consultant."

Thinking back to some other post-retirement cards that included a list of educational degrees following the name, I wrote out "David L. McKenna, B.A., M.Div., M.A., Ph.D." Then, for the fun of it, I added the letters of honorary degrees, "LH.D. LL.D. D.D." etc. What an ego trip! If I took that route, my business card would confirm the conclusion of a critic who said that Christians were trying to win the world by degrees! Finally, I was saved from myself by remembering my own words in the book *Retirement Is Not for Sissies*:

"Count on it. Exposure of the naked self comes to all of us when the work ends, the position goes away, and the title gets removed. The proof is on our business card. When it reads nothing but our name, our identity has to stand on its own."[3]

Taking my own advice, I cancelled my order for a business card and struck out as a daily walker along the lake and through the village of Kirkland as a man without a title. I was just plain "Dave."

A remedial course in humility followed. I learned what my friend Glandion Carney meant when his international speaking ministry fell victim to Parkinson's disease, "In the school of grace, we start all over again in kindergarten."[4] For me, simple lessons in living that can never be taught by formal education or caught in a professional career were learned on the streets of Kirkland day by day. After ten years on the streets, I find my own words confirmed, "In retirement, our core identity, independent of titles and roles, is set free to grow."[5] Let me tell you why.

# Part I

# Rules of the Road

# 1

## Get A Dog

*"Happiness is a warm puppy"*

—Charles Schultz[6]

Before retirement, I had little time for family dogs. Taffy, the Poodle, and Muffin, the Maltese, hardly knew me. Jan and the kids fed, bathed, and walked them. When Taffy rolled in the carcass of a sea lion on the beach at Camp Casey on Whidbey Island, I made the executive decision to give her away rather than clean her up. When Muffin lost control and started to ruin the carpet in the President's home, it was Jan who had her put down while I was away.

After retirement we were dog-less until Jan made the mistake of checking the want ads for Maltese puppies and telling me about it. I assumed that her interest in a puppy was my command. Christmas was just ahead and I envisioned a little Maltese as her surprise present. So, in conspiracy with our daughter Suzanne, we found a litter at a breeder on the Olympic peninsula. Sue and Sean, her youngest son, took the ferry to Bainbridge Island, met the breeder at the dock, and then secreted little Molly under her coat for the ride home. On Christmas Eve, we gathered as a family and prepared for the ritual of opening presents. With anxious grandchildren chomping at the bit, Suzanne said, "Mom has to open her present first." When Jan opened the top of a big box wrapped in

Christmas foil, a little white ball of fuzz jumped out and into her arms. Without hesitation Jan dubbed her "Miss Molly McKenna."

After the party we took Molly home for her first night in the McKenna household. Together, Jan and I pledged that Molly would be appropriately trained and disciplined. I put her in a kennel in the laundry room and went to bed. Pitiful little cries punctuated by yips kept us awake until midnight. Our resolve melted and we agreed that we would bring her to bed with us for "just one night." As soon as I picked her up and put her between us, she snuggled right into the crook of my arm. Yes, you guessed it. Fifteen years later, that's where Molly sleeps. She won my heart and became "Daddy's dog."

Five years later Molly and I joined the scores of people who walk on Lake Street around Marina Park and up the hill to Park Place in Kirkland. It's a dog world. Do you remember how Garrison Keillor opened his show, *The Prairie Home Companion*, at the Paramount Theater in Seattle? He rubbed his chin and mused, "Hmmm. So here we are in Seattle, where there are more dogs than Christians." If you count the number of people and the number of dogs walking on our streets during church time on Sunday morning, he might be right. His humor, however, leads us to an ominous note. Facts show that there are actually more dogs than children in the City of Seattle. Are we missing a message?

I want to tell a different story. Molly, our Maltese, is the great connector for us as we walk along the street. She is also what I call the "girl magnet." You would be surprised at the beautiful young girls who stop to pet Molly and tell me how cute she is. Molly is also the "widow magnet." Older, single ladies will stop to gush over Molly and start a conversation with me. It really works until I look up and say, "Oh, here comes my wife." How quickly the conversation ends.

Justification for my spiritual connection with Molly comes from such Christian notables as Iraneus, St. Francis, Martin Luther, John Calvin, John Wesley, C.S. Lewis, Billy Graham, and Pope Francis. Each of them gives an affirmative answer to the question, "Will there be animals in heaven?" St. Francis contended that animal souls are eternal and preached a sermon to birds beginning with the greeting, "My sister birds . . . ."[7] In his sermon on "General Deliverance," John Wesley left no doubt about his belief in the "eternal soul of animals."[8] C.S. Lewis went so far as to suggest that animals take on the immortality of their human master just as we take on the immortality of Christ, our Master.[9] Coming up to date, when a man asked Billy Graham if dogs would be in heaven, he answered, "God will prepare everything for our perfect happiness in heaven, and if it takes my dog being there, I believe he'll be there."[10] Most recently, Pope Francis stayed true to the name of his patron St. Francis of Assisi when a little boy asked him if his dog who had just died would be in heaven. The Pope assured him, "Paradise is open to all God's creatures."[11]

When it comes to dog theology (dare I call it "dogma"?), I often cite the musings of Charles Schultz of *Peanuts* cartoon fame. According to Robert Short, author of *The Gospel According to Peanuts,* Snoopy, the beagle hound, is a "little Christ." He is not perfect. Snoopy has his questions about fairness in the world and in his imagination conceives of himself as an Ace flying his Sopwith Camel in dogfights with the Red Baron. From the roof of his doghouse, he watches the stumbles of Charlie Brown, the shenanigans of Lucy, the putdowns of Linus, the woes of Peppermint Patty, and the exasperation of Schroeder with the "wonderful qualities of love, loyalty, watchfulness, and courage." Add to these qualities of character the virtues of "complete obedience and humility at the feet of the his Master."[12] Deepest yet is Snoopy's love for his supper dish and the assurance that it will be filled at dinnertime. George Hegel, the philosopher, reasoned that if the "core of religious faith was the feeling of 'absolute dependence'" then "of all creatures the most religious must be the dog."[13] Doesn't this image give added meaning to the words of the Canaanite woman who countered Jesus' refusal to heal her demonic daughter with perhaps the greatest declaration of faith, "Yes, Lord, but even the dogs eat the crumbs that fall from their Master's table." (Matt. 15:27)

I am biased, but I see in Molly these spiritual qualities that point to immortality. She loves everyone, whether old men pushing walkers or Muslim women peeking through a slit in the veil over their face. With me, she never wavers in her loyalty and she is always ready to forgive me when I leave her or scold her. Utter consistency guides her life. Her pattern never varies from the daily routine of walking, eating, sleeping, and playing. In between she has an uncanny sense of every signal that we send without words to her. Time and time again, Jan and I marvel at her intuition, shake our heads, and ask each other, "How does she know?" Before we can speak it, Molly knows when we are thinking about going for a walk or a ride. With precise timing of her body clock, she appears like Snoopy at her supper dish and rattles it for emphasis. When we take her to visit our children or friends for dinner, she is very patient and stays out of sight until the witching hour of nine o'clock arrives. At that appointed time she appears with authority in her eyes and gives one commanding bark that leaves no doubt. It is time to go home. Or, reverse the process when we go out for dinner or shopping and leave Molly home. Her greeting upon our return is like a family reunion. She runs around in little circles, squeals, and goes back and forth from Jan to me getting a hug and giving a little wet kiss. If, however, we stay out too long, we are in for a scolding with barks that say, "You're late and I don't like it." For me, the most beautiful moment comes when she knows that I am sick and will bring the comfort of cuddling up in the crook of my arm as I lie in bed.

No longer do I doubt the word that a dog adds seven years to our lives. Of the eighteen years since my triple-bypass, I know that I owe at least seven of them to Molly. She keeps me calm and teaches me the meaning of consistency. If I scold her, she asks forgiveness. If I fail to pet her, she just hangs around until I pay attention. Without apology, I told a security officer in the mall that Molly was a "service dog" when he tried to expel her.

Of all the lessons I learned from Molly, the meaning of trust will never be forgotten. Each time that we take her to the vet for an examination or for boarding while we are on vacation, she begins hyperventilating and shaking even before we get in the car. Once we arrive at the doctor's office, however, she settles down and resigns herself to the fact that we will leave while she has to stay. In the vet's arms she looks at us with eyes of trust and waits for us to say, "We'll be back soon, Molly." Jan always cries a little at those times and I feel the empty spot that only Molly can fill. More than once on our annual vacation, Jan and I confessed that we were ready to cut the time short and go home to get Molly.

Molly has aged with me. Chronologically, I am 86 years old and Molly is almost 15. But remember, each dog year equals seven human years. Our grandson, Ryan, figured it out. On December 3, 2014, Molly was 100 dog-years old and we celebrated her centennial birthday.

But Molly is only the start of this streetwalker's story. When a taxi driver in New York City was asked what he loved about being a cabbie, he answered, "It's not just the driving I love – it's the people I run into." That's the way it is with Molly and me. It's not just the walking we love, it's the people we run into. For a start, we can name some of the people and puppies of Lake Street with whom Molly and I immediately connected:

Virginia and *Nick*
Diane and *Mo*
Beatrice and Abby
Claudie and *Rusty*
Casey and *Riley*
Frank and *Ronnie*
Dione and *Pedro*
Christine and *Mac*
Monty and *Bianca*
Dick and *Ika*
Marian and *Angus*
Betty and *Cupcake*
Darlene and *Roxie*
Tommy and *Max*
Lee and *Cory*

So, if you love to run into people, get in step, and take a walk with us. Molly will show the way.

# 2

---

# Take A Walk

*"An early morning walk
is a blessing for the whole day"*

—HENRY DAVID THOREAU[14]

BEFORE RETIREMENT, I FUNCTIONED at two speeds – a fast walk to get someplace and a three-mile run to get my exercise. After retirement, I no longer needed to hurry from door to car or from office to meeting, and, after a heart attack, I could no longer keep the pace of an eight-minute mile on a three-mile course. In their place, I discovered the soul-cleansing value of a leisurely stroll and the physical benefits of walking three miles at an eighteen-to-twenty-minute clip. Join Molly and me on the first walk I have ever taken in which I paid attention to the beauty along the way rather than rushing headlong toward a given goal with blinders on.

When Molly and I step outside our condo for our daily walk, we have the option of going north or south along Lake Street. Instinctively Molly leads the way by turning right and heading north toward the village of Kirkland and Marina Park where she loves to romp. Other than returning home an hour later, we have no other destination in mind. Both of us pay attention to the sights, scenes, and smells along the way. Molly specializes in sniffing the grass, bushes, and posts where other dogs have left her a message. I mark the route by the sculptures along the way that give the village of Kirkland its distinctive character.

Our walk begins immediately in front of our condo, where a waterfall cascades over rocks and spills into a pond attended by the bronze statue of a Native American princess who holds a plate with the symbol "S" for Shumway, the name of the pioneer Kirkland family whose mansion occupied the site where our condo now stands. Without exception, Molly makes a quick potty stop on the manicured lawn directly across from the statue.

Gingerly dodging traffic, Molly and I cross Lake Street into David Brink Park with its two layers of walkways along Lake Washington. Looking back, we can see that water from the falls and pond at the Shumway flows under the sidewalk, ripples down a run between two smaller pools, and under the road to surface again in a tiny pool at the feet of three life-size figures. Bronze-green statues of Native American women clothed in native dress are introduced on a plaque as "The Waterbearers." Each woman holds a jug of water – one dipping to fill it, another pouring it out, and the third carrying it on her head. While I stop to look at the trio, Molly pays no attention to them. She brings to mind a well-known painting that my grandmother had in her home – a Native American on a horse with his arms raised in worship of the setting sun. His horse, however, has its head down nibbling grass. My grandmother told me, "That's the difference between humans and animals. Humans can appreciate the beauty of nature and worship the God of creation while animals cannot." Her lesson comes back to me again and again as I remember sitting on our second-story deck overlooking the sculpture and watching so many walkers stopping to take a picture while their dogs are impatiently pulling at their leashes and wanting to move on.

Molly wins and off we go toward downtown Kirkland. One long block brings us to a stainless steel sculpture entitled "Reverb" that stands two stories tall against the corner of Anthony's Restaurant. Whether in the slightest breeze or the highest wind, vertical mobiles turn silently in exquisite balance with the echo of reverberations from which the sculpture gets its name. Even though the blades are barely turning, I stop, close my eyes, and block out the street noise, hoping to hear the whisper of that sound before moving on.

Molly has something else in mind. She knows that we are heading for Marina Park where she can romp on the grass. So, with the exception of a quick check at the door of BooBoo Bakery and Boutique for dogs, she lowers her head and drives forward past the stores, around the corner, and down the drive to the grass at the park. While she is doing her thing, I note again "The Homecoming" sculpture that I first saw in San Diego many years ago. In bronze the artist has captured all of the emotions of a sailor coming home to the arms of his lover. Each time I pass the sculpture I see those feelings in greater depth as I stop to study the artist's message in the eyes, lips, hands, and feet.

Molly has other ideas. Marina Park is a mecca for dogs. Off she goes only to halt, backtrack, and double-check a smell she missed. I cannot help but smile as I remember the lady who came by with her dog, saw Molly sniffing, and laughed, "She's checking her P-mail." Another daily stop comes at the modern sculpture of the Centennial Fountain. When the water flows into the wind, it splashes over the edge and gathers in little pools from which Molly gets a drink. Or, if the day is nice, little children will play in the shallow water in the base of the foundation and give Molly a chance to put her paws up on the edge as if to join them.

Just past the fountain, Molly always takes a shortcut across the lawn in front of the "Puddle Jumpers," bronze images of six children holding hands and gleefully leaping forward. It is common to see little children joining the jumpers and posing for a picture. At this point Molly 's feet take on speed to climb the hill and head back into town because she knows that a treat is just ahead. On the way, we pass a large piece of bronze art showing two rabbits huddling together under the name "Close Quarters." Nor can we miss looking across the street to check out the "Cow and Coyote," the full-size sculpture of comic relief that greets visitors to Kirkland with a howling coyote standing on the back of a cow. Throughout the year, the cow and coyote are garbed in clothes that celebrate the season, such as Santa hats at Christmas, or which mark a special event in the city, such as the 12th man flag of the Seahawks at Super Bowl time.

Molly, of course, still has other things in mind. Pulling on her leash, she takes me around the corner to the two water dishes outside the Lodge Sports Bar. She tests both of them as if hoping for different flavors and then heads to the crosswalk for Starbuck's where a special treat awaits her. Nourished again, she knows that the next leg of our walk is up Park Lane and past the Howard Mandville Gallery, which has the sculpted figures of a mother and child on a park bench. "Nesting" is the caption for the sculpture. A woman is cuddling a sleeping child on her lap and wrapping her in her arms while holding an open book of an unfinished story.

Another block and I pick up Molly to carry her for a couple of blocks. As she has aged, she has developed arthritis in the shoulder of her right leg so she squeals if picked up the wrong way. Thinking that a three-mile walk, including the hill, might be too much for her, I choose to carry her. When people look and laugh at the sight, I simply say, "Didn't you see the sign that says, 'Please Carry Your Dog?'" I don't hesitate to use it when someone with a big black Lab passes by and looks askance at us.

Once in Peter Kirk Park, Molly is off and running again on a patterned route that takes her up and around the sculpture of "The Gossipers," Picasso-like stick figures of three women in wide-brimmed hats sitting on the ground and huddling together in postures that suggest the whispering of juicy secrets about other women.

It's time to turn around and go home. Molly knows it and picks up the pace as we head downhill, divert through the Kirkland Library just to check on the sculpture of the "Carousel," depicting the happiness of the merry-go-round that I remember as a child, cross back down to Park Lane, make sure that "Fine-feathered Friends," a statue of a little boy feeding birds, is still there, and then turn the corner again at Starbuck's to cross Kirkland Avenue and watch children throw coins into the contemporary "Vessels Grouping Fountain" at the Bank of America building. All of the sniffing is done now. Molly seems to know that there is no more sculpture to see on the way home. Impatiently, she puts her head down and leads me back to the princess at the Shumway falls where she tinkles again in the same spot where we started. As we approach the entry gate to the condo I punch in the code and tell Mollie, "We're home." This is her cue to run up the stairs, across the short hall, and jump up against the door with the hope of pushing it open. She knows that Jan always has a treat of freshly baked chicken tenders in her supper dish.

Our walk is complete for another day. Molly and I will take a nap together after lunch, our bodies toned and our spirits lifted. It may appear as though my itinerary from art piece to art piece is a robotic walk, not unlike that of the automatons who plod ahead with unseeing eyes while listening to their headsets, or the texters who walk right into you without lifting their head. Not so. The artworks are like grace notes for our walk. The real music is in meeting, greeting, and knowing new friends every day. As I said earlier, it isn't just the walking, sniffing, and art that Molly and I enjoy, it is the people we run into.

# 3

---

# Say "Hello"

*Stranger! if you, passing, meet me, and desire*
*to speak to me, why should you not speak to me?*
*And why should I not speak to you?*

—WALT WHITMAN[15]

SEATTLE DOESN'T MAKE THE list of being in the top ten of the friendliest or the unfriendliest cities in America. It does, however, have the mentality of pioneer individualism that keeps people at arm's length from each other and an aura of suspicion based upon limited trust. That's where a dog makes a difference. Only the most callused of streetwalkers can resist the black eyes and wagging tail of a little white Maltese in a Seattle Seahawks rain jacket. More often than not, I am totally ignored or treated as a necessary evil holding the other end of the leash.

As a guy who has been known as "President," "Doctor," and "Reverend," this was more than my exaggerated ego could take. With a little bit of vengeance in mind, I decided to take the initiative by greeting every person on the street with the challenge of "HELLO." I surprised a lot of people, especially those whose ears were plugged by audio nubs and whose eyes were blotted out by sunglasses. The grunts that I got in response led me to rethink the way I say "Hello." First, I categorized the tone of the responses I received. At one extreme I heard a gruff monotone that said, "Don't bother me." At the other extreme a flirty twirl at the end of the world seemed to say, "Don't I know you?" In between I heard "Hello" with the sunshine of a smile that was a good as "Have a great day." So, rather than joining the grunts or the flirts of the street, I decided to say "Hello" or "Hi" to everyone we met with the uplifting voice that neighbors give to neighbors. What a difference it made. In one case a woman jogger refused to raise her eyes to Molly and me even though we passed almost every day. I broke into the glaze with a bright "Hello" and got a surprised look back. Next time around she raised her eyes and showed a smile. A couple days later I was stunned when she lifted her hand for a "high five" as she passed by.

The walking or running automatons with the earplugs gave me a new challenge. Because they had to read my lips to know what I was saying, I worked on facial features to complement the verbal greeting. "Hello," now came with a bright look and a lilting lift for everyone whom I met. Stares of suspicion gave way to smiles of surprise, but not completely. You can tell recent immigrants from other nations who have come to Kirkland to work at Microsoft and Google. At first, they are not sure how to respond, but I found that a bit of attention to their children or babies opens wide the door to a friendly greeting.

How did I respond to those who answered my "Hello" by asking, "How are you doing?" At first I gave the pat answer "Good" or "Great," but then decided that I needed to be creative. A couple times I reached back into family history and pulled out one of the quips by which Jan's father was known when he walked the streets of Spring Arbor, Michigan as the pastoral patriarch of the little community. Naturally, everyone he met asked, "How are you doing, Brother Voorheis?" just to hear him answer, "Finer than a frog's hair" or "I'm still taking my regular meals." These words must belong to another generation. Every time I tried to use them I provoked a look akin to the astonishment of someone who had just encountered the village idiot. Finally, I settled into the upgraded version of "Good" and "Great" by adding "What a great day. Let's make the most of it."

One day I became jealous of Molly. Everyone on the street and around the town knew Molly, but nobody knew my name. This led me to a new tactic. When walkers stopped to pet Molly, I said, "Hello, I'm Dave" and stuck out my hand. It worked. One by one the people on the street, in the shops, and at the sitting areas took on names that tested my memory. Once I heard a person's name I repeated it immediately or as soon as we parted. I also found associations with other names I knew, other persons with the same name, and even comic thoughts that only Jan and I know, such as "Ditzy," "Pa and Ma Kettle," "Busty," "Corncob, " "Grouch," "Go Blue," and "Miss Priss." Much to my surprise, when I got curious about the number of people on the street whom I could greet by name, 97 people came to mind. Old and young, male and female, straight and gay, Caucasian and African-American, Jew, Muslim, and Hindu, no one was excluded. Suddenly, my pastoral heart took over and I realized that I had a small congregation to whom I could minister, even though no one called me "Reverend."

A lesson from the past came back with this new insight. During my seminary years I enrolled in a program sponsored by the Institute for Pastoral Care at the University of Michigan to qualify as a hospital chaplain. After a couple of weeks of intensive courses, we were assigned to a hospital ward, not as student chaplains, but as orderlies and nurse's aides. In our orientation along with a new class of future orderlies and nurse's aides, no one knew that we were graduate students in theology dressed in the same green gowns as other inductees. To begin, the instructor introduced us to our role with the encouraging words, "By the time you finish this training period, you will know the name and number of every bedpan in the hospital." His prophecy proved him right. I shared traumatic experiences in partnership with a young African-American man. Early on, we were asked to prepare an "RC" ("respiration ceased") body for the mortuary. After plugging all of the orifices of the body, I took the feet and he took the head to put the corpse on the gurney. On signal we lifted the body. A deep-throated moan petrified us. I remember looking up at the eyes of my partner. They were scared wide open with white surrounding all of the sheer fright in the black centers. Only later did we learn that persons whose respiration has ceased still retain some air in their lungs that causes them to groan when the body is lifted.

Back to our story. Yes, I learned the name and number of every bedpan. Two tough weeks of orderly duty went by as I tried to serve helpless and hopeless people in the surgical ward of the hospital. One of my patients was a man dying of brain cancer. As his orderly, I found him to be bitter, cantankerous, and vulgar. More often than not, he cursed me when I tried to help him. At the end of two weeks of orderly duty interspersed with classes in the chaplaincy I was given a white jacket with a blue cross stitched on the pocket and my name embroidered above the cross. As my first act in my new role, I went back to the man with brain cancer to re-introduce myself as his chaplain with the hope that I could minister to him as a friend and a pastor. One look at me, my white jacket, and the blue cross transformed him. Instantly, he dropped his curses for blessings and his bitterness for a Christian testimony. What a difference a white jacket and the blue cross can make!

This lesson came back to me on the streets of Kirkland. If I were Molly's Dad or just "Dave" rather then "Dr. McKenna," "President McKenna" or "Reverend McKenna," I had a chance to see people as they were and minister to them with the gentle touch of genuine love. Please, do not take away from these comments any thoughts that I demean the role of an ordained and titled clergy. Quite the contrary. If I had my choice, I would have clergypersons in a clerical collar along with judges in robes and doctors in white coats. The loss of the symbols of authority in our society is a genuine loss. There is the need for ministry at both the formal level of spiritual authority and the informal level of spiritual anonymity. For me, as a streetwalker in Kirkland, Washington, anonymity is an asset.

# 4

## Ask A Question

*"I'm always looking, and I'm always asking questions"*

—ANNE RICE[16]

AFTER THE HUMAN CONNECTION of "Hello" and personal identification of a name, the natural question for streetwalkers is "How are you doing?" Let's be honest. We really don't want to know the answer. But what if we did? Was it curiosity or inspiration that caused me to listen for the answer? Once I did, another world opened up. I learned what Atticus Finch meant in the book *To Kill a Mockingbird*, "You never really understand a person until you consider things from his point of view – until you climb into his skin and walk around in it."[17] Going one step farther, I also discovered what the Quakers meant when they said, "An enemy is a person whose story you have never heard."

### The Caring Question

Dare we listen to the answer that follows the question, "How are you doing?" Here is the reward for listening. A neighbor stopped on the street to say "Hello." I asked, "How are your doing?" He answered, "Fairly well." Usually that would be the end of the conversation. But, in this case, I dared to ask. "What is unwell?" He answered, "My wife's loss of memory is becoming worse." This opened the door for me to walk alongside him through the "dark night of soul" when he had to release his wife to a memory center and go through the agony of being alone for the first time in more than 50 years.

On another morning, I greeted two women who were walking together and wearing matching pink shirts. I perked up and said, "Hi. Are you twins?" "Yes," they answered, "We are both survivors of breast cancer." Later on, I saw one of the women walking alone and asked how she was doing. Gritting her teeth, she said, "The markers are up." Since then, she has made sure that her twin survivor keeps me posted on the torturous path through chemo, radiation, and multiple hospitalizations in her fight to survive.

Are you with me? What greater opportunity for compassionate ministry could ever be given to a clergyperson who walks the street incognito? I could only say to my neighbor whose cancer came back, "We are with you. You have our love. We will pray every day."

# Learning to Listen

Listening is a virtue of leadership that is often commended, but seldom exercised. When push comes to shove, most leaders are lousy listeners. I am the chiefest of sinners. In high school I was an aggressive debater; in college I campaigned for student body office; in seminary I preached sermon after sermon; in graduate school I doubled as a teaching assistant; in my career, I gave lectures, announced decisions, and gave hundreds of speeches on and off campus. Like E.F. Hutton, I assumed that when I spoke, everyone listened. One day, however, I learned to listen. I was co-chair for a magazine called *The Pastor's Personal Library*, a publication offering book reviews to help focus a pastor's reading. My co-chair was Dr. Martin Marty, a man whose scholarly credentials as Distinguished Professor of History at the University of Chicago make my dossier look like a starter kit. In between the give and take of one of our work sessions, Marty and I went to lunch and then took a stroll through the hotel lobby. We passed by the open doors of a room where a tobacco company was marketing its latest packaging as an attraction for younger smokers. Marty stopped at the door, listened to the appeal, and then said, "If only the church had that kind of message." I asked him what he meant and he answered with an impassioned discourse anchored in history and applied to the changing contemporary scene. Wisdom oozed from his words and I knew that I was in the presence of greatness. From then on, whenever we met, I just asked Marty a question and then became silent as he threw open the windows of his knowledge and showed me what I had never seen before.

## Listening to Learn

This lesson in listening became a discipline whenever I had a chance to talk with academic colleagues, religious leaders, and political figures who had knowledge or experience from which I could learn. Looking back upon my experience in the Northwest, I prize what I call "listening moments" in the presence of great minds and souls at local, national, and international levels. Join me as I recall listening to:

- Dan Evans, Governor and U.S. Senator, speaking of his conviction to limit gambling in the State of Washington;

- Charles Odegaard, President of the University of Washington, reflecting on the difference in leverage for leadership between public and private higher education;

- Mary Gates, President of United Way in King Country, remembering her days as a schoolteacher and the joy she found in voluntary civic leadership;

- Earl Palmer, Senior Pastor of University Presbyterian Church, likening "grace of grace" in our lives with the waves of Lake Washington that unceasingly wash against the shore;

- Bob Utter, Chief Justice of the Washington State Supreme Court, telling how Jesus's words of forgiveness led him to the position of wiping the slate clean for a person who was acquitted of a crime;

- Bruce Kennedy, President of Alaska Airlines, envisioning the design of the "Kodiak" airplane for the special needs of missionary aviation in the bush country;

Add to these "listening moments" some of the other encounters that shaped my life and my career;

- John Stott, Rector of All-Souls in London, calling for humility in carrying the case for world Christianity;

- David Hubbard, Fuller Seminary President, musing over a statue of "Blind Justice" in a public square in Lausanne, Switzerland, and noting, "God is just with His eyes wide open" ;

- Mark Hatfield, Governor and Senator, calming my little snit over the failure to be appointed Secretary of Education by telling the story of how he missed being President of the United States by the blink of a political eyelash;

- Lloyd Ogilvie, Chaplain of the U.S. Senate, showing me what it means to be a "pastor to politicians;"

- Elton Trueblood, Quaker philosopher and former Dean of the Chapel at Stanford, who inspired me to search for the "Big Idea" as the vision for a Christian college;

- Elisabeth Elliot, widow of the martyred missionary Jim Elliot, who gave a withering eye to evangelical foolishness;

- Carl F. H. Henry, Editor of *Christianity Today*, who decimated my first manuscript for a published article but encouraged me to keep writing

- Joni Erickson Tada, author, speaker, and quadriplegic by accident, who said, "Hug me, I won't break" when I hesitated to greet her.

- Ken Taylor, Chair of Tyndale Publishers, who walked me through his story of becoming speechless and then left with a permanent stutter while he translated the Bible as the Living Word;

- Ken Hansen, Chair of ServiceMaster Corporation, who honestly told me that my gift of articulation left him wondering about my authenticity;

- Dan Karn, Chair of Consumer's Power in Michigan, who convinced me I could have more influence as a president running a college than as a politician running for Congress;

- Jack Eckerd, drugstore magnate, who had the honesty to say that he wasn't enough of a Christian to give away his fortune . . . . "yet."

- Billy Graham, evangelist, who explained at length why he would not allow a newly-proposed and endowed Christian university to carry his name;

- Ruth Graham, wife of Billy, who shared the story of hurt that Billy felt after being attacked by a religion editor of a Seattle paper during his 1976 Crusade;

- Chuck Colson, Counsel to President Nixon, who proved that he was genuine by sprinkling his speech with "hell" and "damn" in our first conversation after his conversion to Christianity;

- Carl Sagan, renowned cosmologist and avowed atheist, who told me how thoroughly he had studied the Christian faith and confessed that sometimes he had doubts about his disbelief;

- Donald McNichols, Professor of English at Seattle Pacific University, who walked me through his story of being the first of the medics entering Dachau at the close of World War II and being subjected to sights, sounds, and smells that turned his hair white overnight;

- Margaret Mead, anthropologist and recipient of the award from the Pacific Science Center, who looked down from the Space Needle restaurant, asked about the golden dome on the Fifth Avenue movie theater below, and then mused, "Hmmm, there was a time when golden domes were reserved for cathedrals on the highest hills of our cities." [/BL 1-18]

I could go on. Whenever a younger person asks about direction for the future, my first word is "Learn to listen." It is not easy. We may not always agree with what we hear and there will be times when forthright words will hurt or shame us. But, if we view listening moments as teaching times, there is so much to learn. For me, listening to great minds and reading great books are companions in a liberal education.

In retirement, I took the lesson of listening to the street. One of my favorite questions is to ask an elderly person on the sidewalk, "What did you do in your career?" A light snaps on in them and by listening rather than talking I have learned about a WWII pilot carrying nuclear weapons on alert over China, FBI intelligence on terrorists, radiation therapy for cancer, hospice nursing, autistic children, football coaching, exotic birds, art history, and French cooking. At the age of 86, I find my education is picking up speed because I finally learned to turn "How are you doing?" into a listening and learning experience.

# 5

## Hear A Story

*"Many a man would rather you heard
his story than granted his request."*

—PHILLIP STANHOPE, EARL OF CHESTERFIELD[18]

OH, THE POWER OF a story. How many times have you had a radical paradigm shift after hearing someone's story? My favorite is the story that Stephen Covey tells in his book *Seven Habits of Highly Effective People*. A businessman gets on the subway after a hard day at work and looks forward to a quiet moment behind a newspaper on his way home. At the first stop, however, a man with two small children gets on the car and sits right next to the harried businessman. The children are noisy, restless, and disturbing to him. Finally, he asks the father if he cannot control his children. The answer comes back, "We just left the hospital where they were told that their mother is dying. I thought it might be O.K. for them to let off a little steam." Covey needs no other illustration to describe a paradigm shift. The businessman did a 360-degree turn into apology, compassion, and understanding.[19]

### The Critical Question

Jan and I have had a similar experience as we have walked through the park at the Kirkland Marina. At times, we felt as if we had been transported to an alien world because the majority of people who pass by speak another language. Down the sidewalk comes a Muslim woman in black headdress with only a slit for the eyes. Bias kicks in and you want to say, "Don't you people know that you are in America?" But wait, what if we knew her story?

As we walk with Molly toward Marina Park we often meet a tall thin lady coming the other way. She sees us, stops, turns, and asks if we are going to the park. When we answer "Yes," she falls into step with us and follows us all the way to a bench where she invites us to sit down with her. This is the last thing we want to do and therefore develop divertive tactics to either bypass her early or find a reason to hurry on and leave her sitting alone. But what if we knew her story?

A young woman is standing outside a store talking on a cell phone. She wears black jeans and shirt with the accents of spiked hair, looping chains, and visible tattoos on her arms and neck. No apology is made for her sexual orientation. She turns as if to avoid speaking to us but Jan says, "Hi" and a pleasant voice returns the greeting. As we walk on Jan tells me that she is her friend and a Christian who speaks openly about her faith, her prayers and the blessing of God. Our stereotype falls when we ask, "But what if we knew her story?"

# Grace and Truth

Prejudice, even religious prejudice, decreases when we get to know people and their stories. I think of the hot dog man in Marina Park. He appears with his little stand every day that the sun shines throughout the summer. His English is fractured, but his understanding is articulate. Given time he gathers in the words and gets his point across. I learned that his name is Leo and he is a native of Pakistan. Each time I walk by with Molly, he intones, "Hot dog!" Even though I have to tell him that hot dogs are not good for me, he doesn't hesitate to share a few words with me. Through the broken English I learned that he sells hot dogs through the summer in order to support his wife and three children as well as a family back in Pakistan. Our relationship has become so special that we both raise our hands and say, "Hi, Friend" as we pass by. One cool and cloudy day, when the hot dog business was lagging, he left his stand to come and talk to us. With one eye glancing over his shoulder to spot potential customers, he pulled out his billfold to show us pictures of his family. I asked his wife's name and he answered, "Pretty." Pressing on, I asked if he had pictures of his three children and he proudly pointed out the two who are students at Western Washington University and the younger one who is still in high school. As he flipped through his pictures I noted one that showed him in a military uniform with three stars on the shoulders. Leo explained that he retired as a Captain from the Pakistani army after 17 years of service and came to the United States for the sake of his children's education. Then, he explained why a man of his note was selling hot dogs in a city park. Leo said, "When the Almighty God comes for me on my last day on earth, I want Him to find me standing." This unforgettable testimony set us free to talk about retirement from the military, deployment at a hot dog stand, and a faith that begins with God and promises that we will be standing when He comes for us. A door opened wide for deepened friendship and spiritual conversation. Despite what the doctor says, I am going to buy one of his hot dogs.

So, you see, whether we are talking to Christians, Muslims, Jews, homosexuals, or atheists, our perception changes when we know their story. In their book, *American Grace*, Robert Putnam and David Campbell take on the question, "How has America solved the puzzle of religious pluralism – the coexistence of religious diversity and devotion? And how has it done so in the wake of growing religious polarization?" Their answer is very practical and very problematic. They conclude, "By creating a web of interlocking relationships among people of many different faiths. *This is America's grace*."[20] How does this apply to a person of Christian faith taking a daily walk in a secular city and making friends with people of racial, ethnic, moral, and religious diversity?

Jesus gives us the answer from the example of His own life. In the Gospel of John, Jesus is introduced as the "*. . . one who came from the Father, full of grace and truth*" (John 1:14). Grace and truth are twin virtues of character that define our Christian faith. Too often, however, we assume that truth leads and grace follows. When we take this stance we compound the current climate of divisiveness identified by Martin Marty as a time when "People who have strong convictions these days are not very civil, and people who are civil often don't have very strong convictions. What we need is 'convicted civility.'"[21] Isn't this how Jesus is introduced to us? He led with grace and followed with truth – convicted civility at its best.

Phillip Yancey reminds us in his book *Vanishing Grace* that Christians throughout history have been change agents in hostile cultures when they are led by the grace of giving, serving, and sacrificing for the needs of outsiders.[22] Yancey is echoing the wise words of Archbishop Temple who left us this message, "The Church of Jesus Christ is the only agency on earth that is designed to serve others than their own."[23] No one expects those of us who follow Christ to forfeit our convictions about truth, but everyone expects that we will lead with grace.

## Text and Tone

The best expression of grace and truth that I know for a streetwalker is to sound a note of joy and speak a word of hope. Like music, the sound of joy and the word of hope communicate across cultures and among individuals as a universal language. They cannot be artificially contrived or become a deceptive means for carrying out an ulterior motive. Joy must rise from the soul and hope must be an expression of spirit. This means preparation for both soul and spirit. While I make no claim for sainthood, I can say that walking the streets with Molly has made me a different man. In the wakeful moments of the night and early morning I ask, "Lord, if it is Your will, let me sound a note of joy and speak a word of hope for someone today." This is a radical change from my CEO prayers when I asked God to help me solve a problem, deal with a person, or meet a goal for the day. Text has given way to tone.

Boldness now accompanies my questions to friends on the street. One of my favorite tactics after becoming acquainted with a new friend is to look quizzically and say, "Let me see, my guess is that you were a banker (schoolteacher, nurse, computer engineer, etc.) in your other life." Without exception, the flattery works. We all want to talk about ourselves. No one has ever failed to open up and tell his or her story. Even if I miss my guess by a thousand miles, I learn so much more about the person than his or her profession. And here is the surprise. Not once do I recall a friend on the street answering my question and then saying, "But what do you do?" No one has ever heard my story about being a university president unless my ego got in the way and I told it. Every time I did, I regretted it.

# 6

## Be A Noticer

*"Successful leaders, we have found,*
*are great askers, and they do pay attention"*

—Warren Bennis and Burt Nanus[24]

Molly doesn't miss a cue on our daily walk. She instantly knows the difference between a treat and a threat. Susan, the parking enforcement officer, carries MilkBits for Molly along her route and never fails to pull over to the curb to give her the treat. All Molly needs is the sight of the little traffic wagon across the street and she waits expectantly until Susan arrives. With the same sensitivity, she knows the threat of speeding skateboards careening down the sidewalk toward her. A frightened move to the grass gives them wide berth. As usual, Molly knew instinctively what I have to learn by trial and error.

### The Great Divide

Our daily walk takes Molly and me to the end of Park Lane, through the new transit station on Third Street, past the manicured Lee Johnson baseball field, up the hill, and into Peter Kirk Park. At first, I paid no attention to the people waiting for buses at the transit station. Then, I read that the greatest gap in the world between "haves" and "have-nots" is not economic or social, but the difference between persons who drive cars and those who use public transportation. I got a glimpse of that reality the next time Molly and I crossed Third Street at the transit station. We stepped out of the world of Mercedes, Lexus, Audi, and BMW into the world of people without cars waiting for buses. It has its own shock value. The difference is further spelled out in the racial mix, the clothes, the bags, and even the look in their eyes. I felt ashamed because on our travels Molly and I had walked by them without smiling, saying "Hello" or daring to ask, "How's your day?" No more. I now see them as the people whom Christ described as those who will go from last to first at the gates of heaven and strangers for whom He said we are accountable.

# Rolex Watch Time

It took one of the bus people to teach me what it means to pay attention to little cues that tell a larger story. The transit station is an intersection for young people coming from various parts of the area. Groups of them cluster on the hillside and around the Kirkland Teen Union Building in the park. Despite my bias that marks them as rebels because of their grungy clothes, backpacks, hooded jackets, tattoos, and dangling cigarettes, they are always courteous when Molly and I pass by, even taking time-out to turn their heads and say, "We love your dog." It is not uncommon for a teen with a cell phone and a cigarette to ask me for a buck for bus fare. I usually ask if he or she has seen the sign reading "No Soliciting in the Park." Most of the time the young beggars answer, "Have a nice day" and we both go on our way.

On one occasion, however, we met a young man who had just stepped off the bus. He wore baggy black pants that hung below his hips and a black T-shirt with some kind of exotic design on it. One look at me and he broke into a knowing grin along with the exclamation, "Nice watch!" He shocked me speechless. I had telegraphed to him a message of our differences by the watch I wore. A second wave of shock sent a chill up and down my spine. He had also warned me that I was a target for a mugging. As he walked away I couldn't help but admire him. Most of the time, we are not aware of the cues we send by the cut of our clothes, the style of our hair, and even the glint of our watch. He, however, needed just one cue to read me and send a warning. A Rolex is not a Timex.

# Cue Tips

My interest in reading cues goes back to graduate school days. In a clinical course in psychological testing the professor brought in a nine-year old boy to take an intelligence test in front of our class. Afterward, she asked us to write a short paper on everything we noted about the boy as he took the test. When she read my paper she called me into her office and asked if I would switch fields because I had perceived hidden cues in the boy's demeanor that were so valuable to the work of a clinical psychologist. Although I did not change fields, I did learn that sensitivity to the cues of body language, facial expression, and intonation of voice are just as important to understanding the individual as the test itself.

Warren Bennis, a foremost authority on leadership, says that those who excel as leaders are "first-class noticers."[25] Like Moses in the wilderness, they pay attention to the sight of a burning bush where an angel awaits. Or, as I remember reciting Elizabeth Barrett Browning in junior high school,

> Earth's crammed with heaven,
> And every burning bush afire with God;
> But only he who sees, takes off his shoes—
> The rest sit around it and pick blackberries.[26]

The same insight came as I studied the leadership of Jesus in preparation for writing a book called *The Jesus Model*. Throughout the Gospels we see how Jesus was always on the alert for cues related to reading human character or responding to human need.[27] Seeing the little man Zaccheus up a tree, feeling the touch of a desperate woman on the hem of his garment, telling a Samaritan woman that she has had five husbands, taking little children into his arms after they had been rebuffed by his disciples, weeping at the death of his friend Lazarus, and being crushed by the rejection of his beloved Jerusalem leave no doubt that he was a "first-class noticer." The best example of all is when Jesus sees Nathaniel, the skeptic, coming toward him and says, "Here is a true Israelite, in whom there is nothing false." Nathaniel can only blurt out the question, "How do you know me?" Jesus answers, "I saw you while you were still under the fig tree . . . ." Some biblical scholars use this statement as proof of the omniscience of Jesus as the Son of God. The words, "I saw you . . . " counter that interpretation. Jesus is saying that he came to his conclusion by reading the cues of his character from a distance. As the Son of Man as well as the Son of God, Jesus exercised his human powers of perception to know and understand what people were like.

## Reading the Cues

Armed with these insights, I decided to join Molly as a "first-class noticer" on the sidewalks of Kirkland. While walking past Starbucks we spotted an elderly man sitting in one of the chairs outside the restaurant. A casual "Hello" took on meaning when I noticed the new blue cap that he was wearing with the embroidery on the front, "Husky Crew" and showing crisscrossed oars separating the words. I couldn't help but ask, "Did you row for the Huskies?" He lifted his head, straightened his shoulders, and proudly answered, "Yes, I did."

Just a few days before our meeting on the street I had read the best-seller *The Boys in the Boat*, Dan Brown's story of the Husky crew winning the gold medal at the 1936 Olympics in Germany over every obstacle concocted by Hitler to assure a home victory.[28] Genuine curiosity prompted me to ask, "What did you think about *The Boys in the Boat*?" His face took on the look of first-hand experience as he answered, "A great book, although there some parts where I don't agree."

What an invitation to a conversation! We chatted about the book, our careers, our families, and our retirement. The only negative note came when he told about being a therapeutic radiologist working with cancer patients in one of the best- known hospitals in

Seattle and I had to counter by revealing that I had been President of Seattle Pacific University. Just like the man in the cancer ward of the hospital who saw me change from the green gown of an orderly to the white jacket of a chaplain, I felt that our conversation lost its value when I turned it into a game of one-ups-man-ship. I left a new friend vowing never to let it happen again.

Insignia on the caps of men are always worth noticing. After seeing the name "Husky Crew" and the symbol of crossed oars on the cap of my new friend, I decided to pay more attention to the symbols and names on the caps of men who passed by. The minute I made that decision, I noticed caps with names running the gamut from "USS Enterprise" and "P.O.W" to "Maui" and the "U of M." To the last one I shouted, "Go Blue," the cheer of a Michigan alumnus. Of course, the man stopped and we exchanged information about the year of graduation, field of study, career in Seattle, and the chances of the Wolverine football team under its new coach.

Once you begin noticing the telltale clues to human stories of people on the sidewalk, a whole new world opens up. Sayings on T-shirts, crosses on necklaces, tattoos on the body, burkas on the head, silk saris for the body, stiletto heels on shoes, ballet dresses on little girls, hoods on teens, backpacks on kids, football jerseys with Seahawk numbers, twin babies in a tandem stroller, library books under the arm, Mohawk haircuts, expensive stonewashed jeans with ragged knee holes, walkers, canes, and wheel chairs for the handicapped—the list is endless. Each of them is a cue to an untold story. The tendency is to rush to judgment based upon our background and our bias. Stereotypes fall into place so quickly and discrimination raises its ugly head in a thousand different ways. Again, Molly is our teacher. She is a friend to everyone she meets, responds to their voice, and welcomes their touch—all without prejudice. Following her example, we need to remember that every cue is an opening to a personal story that may need to be heard and that we may need to hear.

# 7

## Find A Symbol

*"Symbols are the imaginative signposts of life"*

—Margot Asquith, Countess of Oxford[29]

Picture a white-haired man in his mid-80s lagging behind a younger blonde woman pushing a stroller with a Maltese puppy peering ahead like a captain at the helm of a ship. Jan is the pusher, Molly is the puppy, and I am the laggard.

Off we go, giving Lake Street a sight to be seen. Never will I be caught dead pushing the stroller. I lag behind just enough so that people who want to laugh might think that Jan and I are not connected. Adults along the way make remarks such as, "Well, look at that . . . ," "I've never seen anything like that." and "Oh, how sweet." Little children ask, "Can I pet your doggie?" and toddlers lisp, "Puppy."

We should have a sign on Molly's stroller reading, "Handicapped" for critics whose eyes call us fools. The fact is that the stroller functions as a walker for Jan as she recovers from two back surgeries. By holding the handle and pushing the stroller, she gains balance and can walk farther than she could without the help. At the same time, the stroller prompts all kinds of conversation with other dog lovers. A natural affinity draws us together. We share the names of groomers, learn differences between breeds, and agree that our dogs have become beloved and indispensable members of our families. Once again, personal stories open and anonymous dog owners become friends with names.

We are not the strangest sight on the streets of Kirkland. The other day we saw a man coming toward us being led by an animal that looked like a long-nosed albino version of a vanilla Lab. When he got closer we did a double-take. It is a pig in a blanket with booties on all four feet! Even passive little Molly growls from the safety of her stroller. Strange as it seems, there is not much difference between us. The man is known by his pig; we are known by our stroller.

Symbols speak loudly in answer to the question, "Who are we?" After becoming acquainted with people on the street I am frequently asked, "Where do you live?" Our condo is across the street from David Brink Park on the second floor of a large 72-unit complex called "The Shumway." A historic marker out in front tells the story of the Shumway family, pioneer leaders in the Kirkland community. At one time the Shumway mansion occupied the site where the condos now stand. In 1980, however, the mansion was moved through the streets of Kirkland and north along Market Street paralleling Lake Washington until it was relocated more than two miles away in Juanita Village. The remodeled mansion is now a retirement home and can be seen by curious history buffs.

As I mentioned earlier, the Shumway condos make up a beautiful complex with immaculate frontal landscaping highlighted by a waterfall cascading over a wall of rocks and running under the sidewalk to two smaller pools and across the street to another pool attended by the three bronze statues of "The Waterbearers." Against this exquisite setting a three- story wall of condos with view decks faces the street. Even though the windows are large and the buff color is commendable, the uniformity of the units tends to take away their personality. It is hard to explain where you live.

When we moved from our home on the Sammamish Plateau for the Kirkland condo, we left behind 150 exotic bushes and plants that made up the landscaping for the builder's model that we purchased. As we considered buying the home, I viewed the landscaping with delight and thought, "It will be fun to trim these bushes and keep up the plants." The fun lasted through one season and then we had to hire a landscaper for visits twice a month and an arborist for semi-annual trimming and spraying of the trees. To our great relief, our move to the condo reduced the landscaping demands to nothing and the gardening demands to four flower-pots and three boxwood planters. With a special love for yellow flowers, I made sure the front deck overlooking the lake always displayed our "signature flowers." By rotating mums, dahlias, marigolds ,and primroses throughout the seasons I was able to cover almost every day of the year, even in the rare times of snow. Now, when people on the street ask me where we live I give them the well-known name, "Shumway," tell them to look up to the second deck on the front-side over the entrance and see our yellow flowers, the symbol of brightness even in the grey days for which Seattle is justly (or unjustly) known. With this description I invite them to wave, honk, and yell, especially if Jan and I are sitting on the deck drinking coffee or watching the parade of people walking by. Now, not a day goes by without waves from people on the street and occasional honks from passing cars. When walking through the village it is common to have someone whom we met only once or twice say, "Ah yes, I remember your yellow flowers."

The character of a culture is read by its symbols. Our earlier culture was read by the authority symbols of the clerical collar, the judicial robe, and the white medical jacket. Whether for good or for ill, those symbols are lost in the swirl of cultural change. A sport shirt hanging loose over jeans symbolizes a casual cler-gyperson, an open-collared shirt under a judicial robe makes a judge seem human, and an occasional shirt, a hideous tie, and an identity tag hanging around the neck causes us to do a double-take when our doctor walks into the room. After I had my heart bypass, I was assigned to a cardiologist for continuing treatment. When we entered his office I was shocked to be assigned to a very large nurse in grubby clothes with tattoos up both arms. All of my biases checked in and I mentally noted that she reminded me more of a matron in a prison camp than a nurse in a specialist's office. While she was taking my blood pressure, a muscular black man walked in, his head partially shaved and featuring a little pigtail in the back. I thought "Whew! At least when I see the doctor I will meet someone who looks decent." Right then, the man in the pigtail turned and introduced himself as my cardiologist. I wanted to run, but had no choice. As the doctor and I began our conversation, I learned that he graduated first in his class at Harvard Medical School, excelled as a student of Christian theology, and spent his spare time reading classic literature. Talk about a paradigm shift. He and I became close friends and every future visit included 20 or 30 minutes of conversation about our reading, our thinking, and our faith. I don't ever recall seeing his pigtail again.

Humans are inveterate symbol-makers and the study of symbols is a field of its own. Tattoos, in particular, fascinate me. As Molly and I walk the streets, I see tattoos that cover arms, legs, backs, and necks, each with its own story to tell. My first reaction is revulsion because I fail to see beauty in them. Then, I am distressed by the thought that they assume permanence when people learn, change and grow. I can't help but wonder, "What will tattoos look like when the skin get old and wrinkled?" Yet, I must confess that tattoos, like all symbols, tell a story. If I could sit down with a person whose body was covered with tattoos and ask what each one meant I would probably have another paradigm shift. Again, I fall back on the question, "But what if I knew their story?"

Molly has her own symbols in the coats she wears. A yellow slicker for rain, a warm plaid for winter, a holiday red for Christmas, and a Seahawk jacket for football season all draw comments from our friends on the street. Don and Dottie, our neighbors in the condo, always stopped their car whenever they saw Molly and me walking. A special bond developed when they said that Molly took the place of the little Maltese that they had lost and could not replace because of Dottie's serious illness. Later, when the illness took her life, Don cleaned out the closet and brought Molly a white Ermine coat and a red silk Santa Claus outfit. They were too much for Molly to wear, but from these symbols we learned how Don and Dottie, who had no children, loved their little dog. Perhaps, just perhaps, after we have to leave the condo, there will still be people on the street looking up for our symbol of the yellow flowers.

# 8

## Have A Reason

*"We do what we do because of who we are.*
*If we did otherwise, we would not be ourselves."*

—Neil Gaiman[30]

Sooner or later, when we show that we care, people will ask the question "Why?" In real time, the word of scripture comes forward, "Be ready to give a reason for the hope that lies within you." (I Peter 3:15). If we align our faith with pronouncements of doom or attitudes of superiority, we miss the point. Following the gift of grace, the reason for our faith comes not in judgment or arrogance, but in the evidence of hope.

## The Kissing Tree

Two little dramas illustrate what I mean. One involved my first encounter with a couple of walkers along the lake. Each morning I saw a tall man with a long stride and a small woman with a short shuffle make their way along the lower level of the David Brink Park. As Molly and I walked on the upper level, we had a panoramic view of the scene below. Whenever this couple arrived at a tall and billowing tree along the Lake, they stopped, hid behind it, hugged and kissed.

Leave it to me. I violated their private moment by stopping them one day and saying, " I have watched you and hereby declare that this tree will be known as the 'kissing tree.'" Bill and Amber did not reject me. Instead, they opened a relationship that was reinforced every day on our walk together. I learned that he was a retired airline pilot and together Bill and Amber had five daughters and a son. Every day that we stopped and talked our friendship took on the feelings of family.

One day, however, I missed Bill and Amber on their morning walk with its view of a loving smooch under the kissing tree. They had told me about the neighborhood where they lived but I had no idea how to contact them. Without leaving a trace, Bill and Amber disappeared from our lives.

# The Elliot Tree

The following fall, when our grandchildren, Ed and Amber Blews, asked me to dedicate their first child to God, they choose the kissing tree along the lake as the site for the sacred ceremony. For Christmas, then, we sent out a picture card showing Jan and me holding our first great granddaughter, Elliott McKenna Blews, under Bill and Amber's tree now redubbed as the "Elliot Tree." The Christmas letter that went with the photo told the story of the "Kissing Tree" renamed the "Elliot Tree." When I took the photo and our Christmas letter to Kinko's for duplication, I did a double-take. Just ahead of me at the counter was Amber herself. One look and we fell into the hug of long-lost friends. Sadly, she told me about Bill's death and her move to a nearby retirement center. In response, I showed her the picture of the dedication under her tree and the story behind it. Amber was overwhelmed. She pled, "Can I have a copy of the picture and the letter that tells the story? I want my daughters to know." Of course, Amber got everything she asked for. Now, from time to time as I trudge up the hill and through the park on my daily walk, I see Amber on the arm of her daughter coming at distance. Her shuffling footsteps take on speed when she sees me. Even before we meet, her arms are out in anticipation of a hug. Without hesitation, we speak our common love and faith in Jesus Christ.

# Mr. and Mrs. Santa Claus

Add the story of William and Mary. As Molly and I ambled along the street we often met a little couple who looked like they stepped out of a storybook. Both of them were under five feet tall. When they introduced themselves as William and Mary, I instantly fixed the names in my mind by remembering the College of William and Mary as well as the reign of King William and Queen Mary. The little man was bald-headed and bespectacled with a white beard that reached almost down to his chest. A twinkle in Mary's eye made the story complete. Together, they made their living in retirement by becoming Mr. and Mrs. Santa Claus at Macy's stores and special Christmas events in November and December. As we chatted one day I asked them if they had seen the plaque that Jan and I donated to a bench on the lookout over Lake Washington. It read:

> "AWESOME WONDER"
>
> *God paints a new picture every day.*
>
> David and Janet McKenna
>
> 2008

The plaque has its story. We knew that we would be limited on what we could put on a plaque in a public park so we chose two words, *"Awesome Wonder"* above the sentence *"God paints a new picture every day."* When I showed William and Mary the bench, I first told them about the man who came to clean our carpets. When he looked out the window of our master bedroom overlooking the park, stretching out to the lake, and rising in the west to the Olympic Mountains, he marveled and said, "God paints a new picture every day." Above this sentence, however, we had the words "Awesome Wonder" etched in the bronze for all to see. I asked William and Mary, "Do you know where the words 'Awesome Wonder' come from?" Mary said, "It sounds familiar but I'm not sure." This gave me the chance to sing,

"O Lord, My God, when I in awesome wonder,
consider all the worlds Thy hands have made.
I see the stars, I hear the rolling thunder,
Thy power throughout the universe displayed . . . ."[31]

Once I started singing they joined with me and a spiritual bond was formed. Soon, I learned that the pastor of their church was an Asbury Theological Seminary graduate during the time that we served as President. From then on, Bill always carried a special treat in his pocket for Molly. More than once, I have used the plaque to discover the faith of other streetwalkers or very gently infer the reason for the faith that lies in me. Ill health has taken Bill and Mary off the street, but our faith and common love will never be lost. The plaque on the bench is a daily reminder of the reason for the hope that binds us together.

# 9

## Let Go

*"Letting go means that we stop trying
to force outcomes and make people behave"*

—MELODY BEATTIE[32]

DOGS TAKE WALKS. PRESIDENTS do not. We either run around a track to get our exercise or dash from place to place to make an appointment. Even though we seriously believe in such idealistic things as seeing the vision, stating the mission, and setting the tone for the organizations we lead, presidents cannot escape accountability on the bottom line, in which success is measured by enrollment numbers, balanced budgets, fund-raising goals, and endowment growth.

Two of my most esteemed colleagues in university presidencies died recently. Full-page, four-color tributes to them appeared in the newspaper. Even though well-spoken words were written about their integrity in office and respect in human relationships, the central focus of the articles was on their achievements that could be counted in numbers, size, and growth. They were credited for running fast and getting results. A president who left the legacy of being just a walker would probably be among the nice guys who finish last.

# Learning to Walk

During my days as a president, I don't ever remember taking a walk. Even jogging round and round a quarter-mile track to get in my daily three miles seemed like an exercise in futility. I had to be going someplace, so I always marked out a three-mile course with a destination in mind. Along the way I anticipated the goal of a "runner's high" that would assure me a sense of achievement.

Molly and a wriggly artery changed my expectations. Ten years after a triple bypass our cardiologist found another artery that was 98 percent blocked and a threat to life. A stent was needed, but one could not be inserted because the artery twisted and turned. The life-saving alternatives were diet, medication, and exercise.

Enter Molly. She taught me how to take a walk. All I have to do is say, "Molly, let's walk." With a switch of the tail she heads to the door, spins in a circle and lifts her head anticipating her leash. Once we are out the door she walks with complete abandon. Every moment is a joy of its own. I follow with cluttered thoughts until I learn the lesson she is teaching. A good walk has intrinsic value. It does not need a speed to be read, a time to be set, or a goal to be reached. Perhaps that is why some acerbic wag said, "Golf is a good walk spoiled."[33] The minute we make walking a game and judge its success by our score against par, its intrinsic value is lost. As Molly showed me, the worth is in the walking.

Molly's teaching came home to me when we met a friend coming toward us equipped with a monitor on his belt and an app in his I-phone to record his progress. With pride he showed us a chart of the number of steps he took each day. When he met or exceeded his goal a bar graph registered a bright green, but when he failed to walk his steps the bar graph showed up red. Brushing the screen to show me the brightest of the green he inadvertently stopped on the darkest of the red and uttered, "Whoops." This was all I needed. My walk with Molly would be ruined if I became a slave to a machine.

# A Good Walk

A good walk is free from the pigeonholes of bias, especially in the relationships we develop with people on the street. Molly treats everyone, except black Labs, as equals. She has no ulterior motive when she stops to let an elderly lady pushing a walker or a little child riding in a stroller reach down and pet her. When a group of children come rushing up with the request, "May I pet your dog?" and I answer, "Yes," Molly goes from one to the other without favoritism. Her freedom from bias led me to ask myself, "Is my 'Hello' the same for the Muslim woman in a burqa as it is for a white woman wearing a stylish jacket? Do I talk differently to an unshaven man with tattoos covering his arms than I do to a distinguished gentleman wearing a cap with 'Stanford Alum' on the front? What mindset kicks in when I see one woman wearing a diamond necklace in the shape of a cross and another wearing the six-pointed Star of David? Do I say 'Hello' as nicely to a grubby kid under a hoodie as I do to an athlete in a newly-pressed baseball uniform heading for the ball field?" Every day I encounter similar questions. It takes confession and shame, discipline and practice, but Molly will not let me forget that prejudice is the way to ruin a good walk.

# A Better Walk

Our walk gets even better when we are freed from the need to control the conversation with every person whom we meet. Again, Molly showed me the way by letting those who speak to her or pet her take the lead. Only when she encounters a black Lab or a white Westie does she assert her authority with an angry growl. Dog experts tell me that she is protecting me, not being territorial about her turf. In fact, they say that if she were off the leash she would not act that way. Except for these rare moments, Molly is perfectly content to let the people she meets lead the way.

The lesson applies to the people I meet as well. My natural tendency is to establish my turf, reveal my identity, and take control. The result is the game of one- up-man-ship that no one wins. And, once you start that game, there is no end. So much more is gained when the desire for control is put aside and you let the conversation flow. Even if the other person is a control-freak, our refusal to play the game is disarming. With competition out of the way, the door is open to a genuine peer relationship when we can enjoy each other and look forward our next meeting. I think of the late Don James and his wife Carol, our next-door neighbors. They are icons in Seattle and legends in the world of intercollegiate football. In my first meeting with Don after we moved in, I wanted to let him know that I had served as President of Seattle Pacific University, but Don disarmed me. He bent down to pet Molly and then greeted me as a new neighbor without the slightest hint of his fame. I had no need to compete and easily identified him as a genuine human being without pretense or guile. Carol, his wife, is a whirlwind of outgoing energy, but equally open and approachable as a friend and neighbor. Jan and she enjoy instant chemistry, common faith, and door-to-door gab sessions. There is not the slightest hint that the First Lady of University of Washington football is in competition with the First Lady of Seattle Pacific University. Once we get over the slavish demand for control in our relationships, the door to lasting friendship swings wide open.

## The Best Walk

Best of all, Molly is teaching me freedom from the tyranny of end results. As a college president I had a heavy responsibility for soliciting annual gifts, leading capital campaigns, and increasing the endowment. Ideally, we talk about "friend-raising" as well as "fund-raising." It is an awkward balance. Anytime a college president appears at the door of an alumnus or in the office of the foundation executive, at best, the motive is mixed. At times I found myself detesting my role because any try at friendship might be interpreted as a ploy to get a gift. Political contacts bothered me even more. Both politicians and their constituents take on the mentality, "What have you done for me lately?" a mindset that poisons any chance of a genuine, human relationship. Although I developed many friendships with personal and corporate donors over the years, there was always the specter of end results in dollars that never went away.

When Molly and I walk together down the street, we are free from the taint of ulterior motives. Molly approaches strangers and wags her tail just for the sake of being a friend. She neither needs nor expects anything more. As hard as it is, I try to duplicate her innocence. When I go over the list of almost one hundred persons whom I have met while walking Molly, I can honestly say that there is not one from whom I expected anything other than friendship.

This lesson carries over into the spiritual realm. Early in life, I was taught that I had to win converts to my Christian faith like a frontiersman counting notches on the stock of his rifle. I failed. It took a long time, but I finally learned the wisdom of Francis of Assisi, "Witness for Christ every day, and if necessary, use words."[34] Rather than trying to take over God's role in nurturing His Spirit in human lives, our part is to be fully present and caring for those whom we meet. A walk that is free from the demand for end results gives us this opportunity.

A beautiful, statuesque African-American woman became a friend when Molly and I met her and her dog in Marina Park one afternoon. At first we talked dogs and weather, but later came the question, "How are you doing?" Her story began to unfold. In the midst of divorce, she was pondering her next step. Would she go back to school and prepare for a new career? Could she regain her trust for a future relationship? I chose to listen and encourage her. Soon, her story took on depth as she traced the route and expressed the emotions of divorce and its aftermath. Now, whenever we meet she greets me with a wrap-around hug that might surprise observers who do not know what is happening. Because she knows I care, I can bring a gentle nudge of direction into our conversation, and have no problem adding the promise, "I will pray for you." Without speaking the word, we have "love" for each other and the end result will take care of itself.

Perhaps you can now feel the freedom that Molly and I have found on our walks together. She had the freedom to romp without bias, control, or end results long before I did. But once I learned to let go, I discovered that a walk is as good as a run, if not better, and perhaps even the best of all.

# Part II
# Lessons of the Street

# 10

## Walk Wary

*"We grow too soon old and too late smart"*

—DUTCH PROVERB

MOLLY WAS A WARY walker, especially when we made our way through the crowds at the Farmer's Market in Marina Park. Imagine yourself at ground level with Molly when the feet of gawkers, talkers, and walkers are coming at you from every direction. Add baby strollers and skateboarders to the mix and you will understand why Molly had to be on full alert, dodging the danger of being knocked down, rolled over, or stepped on. Finally, she looked up with pleading eyes that said, "Please carry me." Of course, I did.

Slow learner that I am, the lesson of being a wary walker came with bumps and bruises. For Molly the danger was physical; for me it was personal. In the beginning I assumed that everyone on the street was a potential friend with good intentions. Close encounters of the dangerous kind taught me otherwise. I learned the hard way to be wary.

### Street Rage

"Road rage" has become a common term that we all understand. With the density of urban populations and the frustration of auto gridlock, tempers flare and violence lurks. No one is exempt, even Christians who profess to love others as they love themselves. A policeman pulled over an SUV on a city street and approached a frightened woman driver. While he was checking her license she asked, "Why did you pull me over?" The cop answered, "You were not doing anything legally wrong but when I saw how impatient you were with other drivers and noted the ICHTHUS sign on the back, I figured that this must be a stolen car." Pastors, in particular, take note.

Now, after ten years of walking with Molly I can introduce you to "street rage." My first encounter with this kind of anger came when Molly and I were on the hill overlooking Marina Park and she had to do her duty. Pulling on the leash she went down the steep hill as far as she could and squatted. I had a poopy bag in my pocket and was ready for action, but nothing happened. At that moment a man and woman came across the street. The man took one look at the scene, pulled out his camera and focused it on Molly and me.

"What are you doing?" I asked none too graciously.

"I'm going to wait and see if you pick it up," he fired back with an extra dose of venom and then added, "If you don't I'm taking the picture to the police."

My rage smoldered as well when I said, "Molly is having a hard time. She isn't doing anything."

Keeping his camera trained on us, he sneered in disbelief, "Well, we're not moving until we get a picture to take to the police."

Later, I thought that I should have taken the poopy bag out of my pocket and waved it in his face. Instead, I growled, "What kind of man are you? Don't you have anything better to do?"

For the next couple of minutes we had a standoff to match the O.K. Corral–he with his camera aimed and I with my angry stare. Molly cooperated by doing nothing so he finally turned to walk away with one last threat flung over his shoulder, "I'm taking this picture to the police."

"Go ahead," I tossed after him.

What should have been a friendly "Hello" between a couple with a camera and a man with a little dog turned into "street rage," as ugly as the worst of "road rage."

# Pizza to Go

Another warning comes with the fun I discovered by saying "Hello" to everyone, asking "How are you?" and looking for cues to hear their story. During our daily walk with Molly, my wife and I noticed a young woman who parked her car in front of our condo and then strode back and forth on the other side of Lake Street at a fast pace with her eyes straight ahead. One day our paths crossed as I was walking alone. I said, "Hi!" She responded with surprise and asked her own question.

"Is that your wife who walks with you?"

"Yes."

She acknowledged my response with a nod and walked away.

A couple days later, I saw her cross the street to come over to my side. We met at the grassy corner where I had stopped so that Molly could do her duty. This time she said "Hi" and asked what I did.

"I am retired" was my evasive answer and I followed it with the quick query, "And what do you do?"

With professional confidence, she said, " I am a massage therapist."

Curiosity prompted my next question, "Do you have an office here in Kirkland?"

"No, I work in homes."

"What does that mean?" I asked.

"I go into homes to give massages, bring pizza, and we have a good time."

All of the red flags flew at the top of the mast. With a grunt of acknowledgment I pulled Molly toward me and headed across the street. Shortly afterwards, she disappeared from the street and left us wondering about her story. If she returns, is it possible that we can minister to her? Would we have the emotional strength to absorb her hurt? Do we have the spiritual resources to break through to her need? We may never know.

Her answer ignited the speed of my retreat. With only a shrug of the shoulders, I pulled on Molly's leash and we headed across the street. But this was nothing compared to an experience yet to come.

## Armani to Spare

On a spring-like day in March, our daily walk took us through the village of Kirkland and around Marina Park. Then I left Jan and Molly at the people-watching spot at the corner of Lake Street and Kirkland Avenue and trudged up the hill to Park Place to get in my extra mile. On the way back, I was climbing the little incline next to the Heathman Hotel on Third Avenue when a shiny, new black Nissan SUV pulled to the curb, the passenger window opened, and voice in broken English spoke, "Excuse me, can you help me?"

"Sure," I answered.

"How do I get to the airport?" Seeing the map in his hands, I pointed him back to 85th Street leading to the entry ramp for I-405 and directly to I-5 where signs point the way to the Seattle International Airport.

"How much time will it take?"

"With the traffic, you need about 35-40 minutes."

Reaching up to his visor, he pulled down a passport with a visible boarding pass sticking out the side.

"My flight is at five o'clock."

"That's good. You have plenty of time."

"Thank you so much," he gushed, "I am going back to Italy. Have you ever been to Italy?"

"Oh yes, many times."

"Where?"

"We drove into Genoa from the Riviera and then on to Milan."

"MILAN! That is my home."

"We remember Milan for its Galleria and Da Vinci's painting of The Last Supper."

"THE GALLERIA! My store is right on the second level. I am a fashion designer for Armani and I am here in the United States showing our latest collection. Here is my card." The official-looking business card read:

---

Fashion Designer                                    Milano

# Toni De Aqua
Moda Italia
Collezione

Cell:+393337422014
Address: Via Montenapoleone, 712
Fax:+39052723600
Email: ToniDeAquaFashionIT@hotmail.com

---

Impressed, I responded, "Well, if we ever get back to Milan, we will visit your store."

"Wait, because you are so nice, I want to give you a gift. Meet me across the street at that parking place." He drove through the green light, parked in a 30- minute spot, and waited while I crossed Kirkland Avenue to meet him on the side.

Telling me again how nice I was, he continued, "After I did my trunk showing of the latest Armani designs I had some beautiful pieces left over that I don't want to take back to Italy because the duty is so high. What size do you wear?"

Like a gullible bass lunging for bait, I answered, "Size 43."

"Ah, this is your day." He reached back between the seats and pulled through a leather jacket in a clear plastic bag with the imprinted name, "Emporio," the well-known Armani signature. Laying the bag on the passenger seat he lifted the plastic cover and fingered the leather of a high-fashioned jacket.

"Feel this," he insisted, "Have you ever felt softer leather?" He was right, The black leather left like silk between my fingers.

"It's yours. " he announced, as he put the jacket back into a black cloth bag that was also on the seat and imprinted with the bold letters of "Emporio."

"Thank you." I reached in and started to take the bag out of the car.

"No, no," he said as he pulled the bag back. "I have something else for you."

Again, reaching between the seats into the back he brought out another black leather jacket in a plastic bag. This one had black buttons on it rather than a zipper, but the leather had the same silky and shiny surface.

"Watch this." Taking a cigarette lighter from his center console, he flipped on the flame and ran it across the leather to show that the fabric was indestructible. Then, he put a second jacket into the bag for me. Again, as I reached in to get my prize, he stopped me and with one smooth stroke produced a brown suede jacket from the backseat saying, "Feel. This is antelope leather. You know the antelope?" Of course, I said, "Yes."

"Do you know how much they are worth?" was his next question.

"I suppose about a thousand dollars each," I ventured.

"Ah, my friend, more than that. They cost almost $7,000."

As quickly as possible, I grabbed the cloth handles ready to take my loot and leave. While I was trying to lift them out of the car, the driver reached across and pulled them back down.

"Wait. Do you have a son?" Because our oldest son had just returned from Paris with designer clothes of his choice, I chose Rob, our younger son, to answer, "Yes."

"What is his size?"

"Umm. He is about 6'1 or 2 and 180 or so pounds. Big shoulders."

"Ah, ha, I have just what he needs." Another foray into the back seat produced three identical jackets to the ones he had already given me. After he put them into a separate bag, I again reached in to lift them out. They were heavy and when I tried to hoist them through the window, a hand grabbed them from me and a voice asked,

"Do you wear suits?"

"Sometimes, but I am retired now."

Another sleight of hand into the back seat brought out still another plastic bag with a charcoal suit done in the fabric and stitching that gives Armani its famous name.

"This is too much," I protested and reached for the bags again.

"No, no, no. They are yours. Can do me two favors."

Suspicious now, I asked, "What are they?"

At that instant, my cell phone rang. When I answered, the worried voice of my wife, Jan, asked, "Are you all right? You said that you would be right back."

"Sorry, Honey. I met a new friend from Milan, Italy who sells Armani jackets and suits . . . ."

At those words, I heard a voice from inside the car plead, "No, no, don't say that!"

Gullibility gave way to skepticism. I assured Jan that I was on my way, hung up and challenged him, "What are your two favors?"

"One, promise that you will not sell them."

"O.K. that's easy. What is the second favor?"

"I had to stay longer than I expected and have the extra cost of a hotel bill. You can help me out if you give me twenty percent of the cost of the jackets and the suit."

A quick calculation on twenty percent of his $7,000 claim put his price at $1,400. The scam was exposed and my Scotch blood boiled.

"No," I spoke emphatically, "I will not do that."

Acting surprised, he frowned and said, "You won't?"

"No, I will not."

Almost pathetically, he pleaded, "But why not?"

"Because it is against my principles!"

With that declaration I spun on my heel and walked away.

O.K. I know what you're thinking and I don't blame you. How could I be so gullible for so long? If P.T. Barnum were alive he would use me as proof that there is a sucker born every minute. Again, I confess, it wasn't until I walked away that I realized that I had been victimized by a scam artist. I actually liked the guy and believed that he was honest. As I walked back to meet Jan, however, all of the little cues that I missed came back to haunt me. Why did he lose interest in my directions when I tried to repeat them in detail? Why was I amazed rather than skeptical when he just happened to have my size in leather jackets? How could he upgrade to Rob's size with the same sleight of hand? Wasn't I the ultimate mark when he showed me two sets of the same leather jackets and then added a suit? Why wasn't I smart enough to catch his fear when I told my wife that I had met a new friend from Italy?

Perhaps, most embarrassing for my male ego was Jan's immediate response when I started to tell her the story. "It's a scam," she declared without the slightest doubt. You can tell why I need her intuitive wisdom to balance out my lack of street smarts.

Returning home, I surfed the web for information on scams. Within seconds I had located the "Italian suit scam" and read story after story that matched, almost in exact detail, my experience—asking directions to the airport, telling the tale of presenting a new Armani line of designer clothes, buttering up a nice guy, offering Armani leather jackets and suits as a gift, setting the stage by citing the heavy duty on returning the goods to Italy, putting a high price on the designer goods, and offering a deal on buying the clothes or asking support for unexpected costs. Boom! I had been victimized by a scam touching every major city in the United States. For better or worse, the streets of little Kirkland had come of age. As for me, I now walk the streets with the smarts.

# 11

## Walk Wisely

*"Dogs are not our whole life,*
*but they make our lives whole."*

—ROGER CARAS[35]

WHAT DID MOLLY TEACH me? No one could fool Molly as the scam artist suckered me. Her intuition sniffed out falsehood and she turned away from anyone who faked an interest in her. In contrast to the street smarts that I lacked, Molly had intuitive wisdom that is taking me a lifetime to learn. I have already mentioned her total trust, her forgiving spirit, and her forward look. Now, I want to go deeper into the lessons that she taught me.

First, she taught me the lesson of *simplicity*. After a career that dealt with the complexities of American society and higher education, it would be easy to become trapped in a web of suspicion bordering on paranoia or despair. Molly never fell into that trap. She sifted through the details of her daily life and concluded that her dinner dish, her daily walk, her playful tossing of puppy bites, and a cuddle at bedtime made for a happy life. I am well aware that the greater gifts of human nature take us above and beyond her level of existence, but we cannot deny that there is a beauty in the simplicity that we may have lost in our hectic lives.

Back in the 1950s when I was preparing a questionnaire for my doctoral research, I submitted a draft to my advisor. He took one quick look at it and said, "You should never ask more than one thing in each of your questions. Otherwise, you confuse the reader and get a muddled answer." I cleaned up the instrument, completed my research, and promptly forgot the lesson. For years as a college president, my speeches and sermons had too many points, my letters had too many requests, and my agenda carried too many items. Finally, I realized that a speech or a sermon that focused on a single point had more take-home value than a complicated treatise designed to show off intellectual sophistication. Long letters asking for funds were not as effective as a single page with a specific request. Books prepared for the Board of Trustees with multiple pages of reports and data needed an executive summary for the Board members to read. And a Board agenda had to be planned with priority of place and time given to the most salient issue to be addressed.

Along came email. Verbosity and complexity took their hits. Early on I learned that the most effective emails deal with only one item. Tweets and Twitter require even shorter messages. Simplicity is the order of the day. Attempts to analyze an issue have no business on the social media, but this has its own downside. To accept conclusions without analysis is the making of an illiterate society that is fodder for dictatorship. While our communication needs the discipline of simplicity, our education demands the discernment of complexity. The test is the way in which we deal with paradox, whether in eternal truth or temporal issues. As I age, I am trying to state facts with simplicity while confessing ambiguities with humility. Yes, the imponderables increase with this viewpoint, but so do the simplicities. Molly taught me that simplicity can have as much, or even more power, than complexity.

Second, as a complement to the gift of simplicity, Molly taught me the value of *smallness*. Not only was she a nine-pound Maltese contending in a field of 100- pound Labs, but she had to function at the ground level under the feet of towering humans, around the wheels of twin-sized baby carriages, and past the bumpers of anxious autos at intersections. As I guided Molly through this maze of monsters, I knew how the Lilliputians must have felt in the land of *Gulliver's Travels*.

I too started out small, trying to wend my way through the footsteps of giants. A forced marriage attended my birth, a Great Depression shaped my childhood, a radical holiness church puts its stigma on my youth, average ability restricted my athletic choices, and limited resources influenced my educational decisions. From that level I was always looking up to those above me. Yet, when I found my niche for bigger things, I began to excel. As I anticipated the completion of my PhD I became captivated by Daniel Burnham's advice, "Make no small dreams, they have no magic to stir men's blood."[36] In our first college presidency in the small village of Spring Arbor, Michigan I led the way in the search for the "Big Idea" that would guide the development of a start-up college, including the commitment to "The Village Is Our Classroom." In our second presidency we moved to a small college in the urban metropolis of Seattle, Washington and I proposed that we follow "The City Is Our Campus." In our third stop at Asbury Theological Seminary, located in the small town of Wilmore, Kentucky, I reached back to the vision of John Wesley and announced, "The World Is Our Parish."

With retirement, however, everything changed. Although I could still dream big, I had no institution through which to project my ideas. Writing books became the major vehicle for continuing to think big. My goal was a book a year until aging started to take its toll on my energy and more and more time became devoted to getting well and staying healthy. As time went by, "big" gave way and I joined Molly in her small world. Rather than settle into a funk, I remembered a book that had captured my imagination back in the 1970s, entitled *Small Is Beautiful*. With this title, E.F. Schumacher, the author, countered the prevailing themes that "growth is good" and "bigger is better." Foreseeing the impact of new technology based on these themes, he proposed a counter-system of economics whose "aim ought to be to obtain the maximum amount of well-being with the minimum amount of consumption."[37] Of course, Schumacher was labeled as a radical with a socialist bent, but his prophetic warnings about "growth is good" and "bigger is better" at the expense of human beings are shockingly true today.

The social media are exceptions. With small technology and minimum consumption, people across the world are being empowered even while the jury is still out on whether or not the end result will also contribute to their wellbeing.

We cannot give up our big dreams when we retire, especially the dream of eternity in the presence of Christ, but the reality of aging dictates that we scale down those dreams to a manageable size. The case needs to be made for small dreams that lead to small wins. I begin each day with a "To Do" list with priorities for action. Highest priority goes to the names of family, friends and neighbors for whom I should pray followed by the pledge to write at least a page or chapter in a new book, spend conversational time alone with Jan, meet a new friend on the street, catch up on emails and appointments, do a household chore for Jan, get in a three-mile walk, attend a grandson's soccer game or band concert, and especially ask God to let me meet someone to whom I can show the love of Christ. Small dreams to be sure, but they are small wins when the dreams come true. Thanks to Molly, small *is* beautiful.

Add *stillness* to the lessons I learned from Molly. Once I got momentum for academic and career achievements my name was "Hurry." I breezed through my senior year in college while serving full time as the pastor of a small church, finished three years of seminary in two years, added a master's degree in two more years, and walked across the stage to receive a PhD just two years later. All of this while being married, having children, and working full-time as a professor and dean. With the same click of the fast-forward button, I planned my career in five-year steps, ever moving upward to some new venture. While I do not remember feeling discontented during those years, I do know that I always had to have the pull of a new challenge, either external or internal.

Stillness of soul is not a memory of those years. My daily devotions were speed sessions and spiritual retreats were avoided like the plague. As my father watched me run, he saw danger in my direction and sent me this verse as his prayer for me:

## WALK WISELY

Slow me down Lord
Ease the pounding of my heart
by the quieting of my mind.

Steady my hurried pace
with a vision of the eternal march of time.
Give me amid the confusion of the day,
the calmness of the eternal hills.

Break the tension of my nerves and muscles
with the soothing music of the singing streams
that live in my memory.

Help me to know the magical restoring power of sleep.

Teach me the art of taking MINUTE vacations,
Of slowing down to look at a flower,
to chat with a friend,
to pat a dog,
to read a few lines of a good book.

Slow me down Lord
and inspire me to send my roots
deep into the soil of life's enduring values
that I may grow toward the stars of my greater destiny.

—WILFRED A. PETERSON[38]

My father never lived to see his prayer answered, but the verse haunted me from time to time through my career. Even retirement came in a hurry. At the age of 65 with the potential for more good years in presidential leadership, I walked away in favor of writing and consulting.

Then I met Molly. It is easy to understand why a puppy can add seven years to your life. Molly calmed me down and taught me to be still. Breeders of Maltese puppies emphasize the importance of an established routine in their lives if you want to assure a contented dog. Can the same be said for a human being who is an

Alpha Dog? I am a case in point. In a very real sense, Molly took control of my life when I fell into her routine. A morning walk, a daily meal, a guaranteed treat, a nap together, another walk, a ride in the car, and a snuggle at bedtime. Best of all, I remember how she sauntered and sniffed on our morning walks along the lake. Without exception, I found myself singing hymns and songs that were hidden just below consciousness. Words and verses that I had learned in childhood and youth came back to me with amazing accuracy and I found that the hymn of the morning always set the tone for the day and kept me singing. Now, I prize the time of stillness beginning with the first moments of wakefulness and finding other moments throughout the day. As a result, the verse of hymn that used to be a drag when singing or reserved for funerals is now one of my favorites:

> Be still, my soul; thy God doth undertake;
> To guide the future as He has the past.
> Thy hope, thy confidence let nothing shake;
> All now mysterious shall be bright at last.
> Be still, my soul, the wind and waves still know
> His voice who ruled them while He dwelt below.[39]

As I sing, Molly looks up at me as if she knows. My father's prayer has been answered.

# 12

## Walk Worthy

*"We give dogs time we can spare,*
*space we can spare, and love we can spare.*
*And in return, dogs give us their all.*
*It is the best deal man has ever made."*

—M. ACKLAM[40]

MOLLY LOVED COMING HOME. When I opened the gate at the end of our walk and announced, "Molly, we're home," she shifted into high gear. Racing up the steps, crossing the hall, and leaping against the door, she knew that she was home.

Easter 2015 is the beginning of a homecoming story. At 3:30 a.m. Molly awakened us with a piercing cry of pain, threw herself off the bed, crashed into the armoire, and collapsed on the floor as if she were dead. I picked up her limp body, felt for a heartbeat, and told Jan, "She's gone." Then another spasm and yelp of pain threw her from my arms and to the floor again. Confused movement took her into the bathroom where she sprawled on the floor with her back legs immobilized, whimpering pitifully. As we knelt with her and stroked her head, we felt paralyzed by helplessness. Minutes passed and then she settled down with black eyes staring as if in a trance. Jan stayed with her while I searched the web for 24-hour emergency animal service. Again, waves of helplessness passed through us as we weighed our options. Before we could come to a decision, however, Molly surprised us by regaining her functions and falling into sleep. She slept through the rest of the night and seemed to be her old self when I took her out in the morning to go potty. On return, she raced for the treat in her bowl and gobbled it down as if nothing had happened. Rather than taking her to the veterinarian we decided to wait and watch her carefully for any further signs of trouble.

Four weeks went by without incident. Except for being stone deaf and sometimes confused, Molly rode in her stroller down to the Marina Park and then jumped out to take command of the park, greeted her people and puppy friends, and took a little nip at a couple of shaggy dogs that challenged her. Whenever she encountered a new dog of her size I used the tactic of saying, "That's a puppy, Molly." Somehow, it appealed to her maternal instinct and she only nudged them nose-to- nose. People who stopped us to pet Molly marveled at the fact that she was almost 15 years old because she still had the puppy look and bounced across the grass when she ran to catch up with Jan pushing the stroller.

Exactly four weeks later, her second seizure awakened us in the middle of the night. The pattern was the same, but the violence escalated. After the first attack, she ran blindly in circles, lost bodily functions, and tried to hide in closets and under shelves. We panicked because the seizure was more severe and we were more helpless.

Many times during Molly's lifetime we had vowed never to let her suffer. Now, our vow came to the test. After she settled down, Ed Blews, our son-in-law and Debra, our daughter, drove us to Companion Animal Hospital. Molly sat erect on my lap, at high alert for any black Labs along the way. This added to our dilemma. We knew that we could not handle another seizure but neither could we bear the thought of losing Molly, especially when she seemed to show signs of spontaneous recovery.

Once we arrived at the hospital we were relieved to learn that Molly's veterinarian, Dr. Valerie Hargett, was on Saturday duty. She took Molly immediately into the examining room and listened to our story. The moment she put Molly on the examining table another seizure shook her little body and another soul-shaking cry spoke her pain. After she settled down, Dr. Hargett examined her and quickly saw the symptoms of a brain tumor. She then explained how the electric shock of pain caused the seizures and how the brain recalibrated after the shock to quiet her down again. With clarity and compassion, she gave the options in such cases and then concluded with the words, "Molly has given you the ultimate gift of love." Through tears Jan and I asked, "This means that we have to let her go?" Dr. Hargett said, "Yes, it is best for Molly and best for you."

The doctor then took us through the process of passing for Molly. She would be given a sedative to put her to sleep followed by an injection that would stop her heart. She asked if we wanted to be present and we both said "No." We were also given the option of receiving the ashes. Again, we said "No." We felt as if we needed to bring closure at the moment, but we did agree to receive her paw print in a plaster memento later on.

Earlier, I told how Molly always looked at us when we left her at the hospital for treatment or boarding. Big black eyes showed unconditional trust as she watched us go and heard the words, "We will be back, Molly, be a good girl."

As long as I live, I will never forget that same look in her eyes as she was held in the doctor's arms and waited for the familiar words. It was almost more than we could take as we cried through tears, "Goodbye, Molly" and turned to walk away. The lesson of total trust has never been harder to learn. I wanted to opt for phenobarbital treatment in order to have her for a few more days. At the same time, I knew that neither of us would survive another nighttime episode. The doctor had it right when she said, "Molly has given you the ultimate gift of love." After a lifetime of preaching that the highest order of love is self-sacrifice for others, Molly filled shallow words with deep meaning. She sacrificed herself for us.

Jan and I continue to walk together down the street and through the village. Not a day passes except our friends and even strangers stop to ask, "Where's Molly?" Tears are shared on street corners and park benches as we give them the news and tell a bit of the story. We now realize how much Molly served as the link between us and the many friends whom we now knew by name. On the morning walk she introduced us to Virginia, Diane, Dick, Carol, Darlene, Pat, Dione, Claudie, Scotty, Casey, John, Cynthia, Beatrice, Steve, Marsha, Lee, Tommy, Mike, Brenda, Heather, Bette, William, Mary, Bill, Amber, Linda, Mark, Katie, Mike, Dorothy, Don, Dotty, Ron, Bonnie, Helen, Gary, Carlene, and Andrew. Through the streets of the village and on into the park, she had such special friends as Georgie, Barry, Theresa, Pam, Vince, Wendy, Kelly, John, Ai, Christine, Tina, Kammie, Jennifer, Betty, Denise, Jack, Yvonne, June, Leo, Ginger, Vicki, Susan, Kathy, Armanda, Lee, Roxanne, Annie, Cindy, Amy, Celine, Mary Jane, Dorothy, Dick, Sue, Bob, Darlene, Rochelle, Trent, and of course, Susan, the traffic officer, who made cars wait while she gave Molly a special treat.

From these friends we hear the common question, "Will you get another dog?" It is too soon for Jan and me to answer the question. At present, we are reframing our lives without Molly. Little remembrances keep reminding us of the hole that only Molly could fill. In our mid-80s, the thought of training a puppy and being trained by one is a formidable challenge. So, for now, we want to say thanks to Molly for giving us the gift of ultimate love. After we created the plaque on the bench in David Brink Park in 2008, we realized that we should have included Molly with our names. It is time to make the correction and honor Molly so that she will be remembered by all of the friends she made for us. Our new plaque on the park bench reads:

> "AWESOME WONDER"
>
> *God Paints a New Picture Every Day*
>
> David, Janet, and Molly McKenna
>
> 2015

# *In Memoriam*

### Paw Prints in My Heart

As I look in your trusting eyes
to say my tearful last goodbyes,
I find it hard to let you go.
You're such a part of me.

The years we shared are now a blur
since you were but a ball of fur.
I still can see you in my mind
unleashed and running free.

But now you're sick and not yourself.
I grieve to know you've lost your health.
Yet you brought boundless joy to me.
I hope somehow you know.

And as I stroke your shiny coat,
a lump grows large within my throat.
I wonder if you understand
this really is farewell.

You look at me as if to say,
"Just stay with me. Don't go away."
And so I will, my little one
as you lay down to sleep.

And though the time has come to part,
you've left your paw prints in my heart.
A heart that breaks imagining
my life when you are gone.

—Greg Asimakoupoulos

*Good night, Miss Molly*

# Notes

## Introduction

1. Colin Powell, quoted in Harari, *A Leadership Primer,* govleaders.org/Powell.htm

2. Miller, *Plain Speaking,* 228.

3. McKenna, *Retirement Is Not for Sissies,* 23.

4. Carney with Brooks, *The Way of Grace,* 12.

5. McKenna, *Retirement,* 24.

## Chapter 1

6. Schultz, *Happiness Is a Warm Puppy.*

7. St Francis, "My little sisters, the birds . . . " www.historyplace. com/speeches/st.fran.htm

8. John Wesley, *"The General Deliverance,"* Sermon 60 (1782) Wesley.nnu.edu/ . . . /sermon-60-the-general-deliverance/

9. Lewis, *The Problem of Pain,* 63.

10. Billy Graham, www.brainyquotes.com/quotes/quotes/bil-lygraham390334.html

11. Pope Francis, www.eonline.com/ . . . pope-francis-confirms-paradise-is-open-to-all-of-god-s-creatures.

12. Short, *Gospel According to Peanuts,* 103.

13. Hegel, *Lectures on Philosophy of Religion,* people.bu.edu/ wwildman/bce/mwt-themes-460-hegel.htm

# Chapter 2

14. Thoreau. "A Week on the Concord and Merrimac Rivers," en.wikiquote.org/wiki/Henry-David-Thoreau

# Chapter 3

15. Whitman, *Leaves of Grass.* www.bartleby.com/142/13/html

# Chapter 4

16. Rice, www.quotehd.com/quotes/Anne-Rice-Author-Quote

17. Lee, *To Kill a Mockingbird,* 30.

# Chapter 5

18. Stanhope. www.goodreads.com/quotes/28396-many-a-man-would-rather-you-heard-his-story-than-granted-his-request

19. Covey, *Seven Habits,* 38-39.

20. Putnam and Campbell, *American Grace,* 550.

21. Paulon, "A Call for Convicted Civility" (June 17, 2013), Townhall.com/ . . . /2013/06/17/a-call-for-convicted-civility -n1620233

22. Yancey, *Vanishing Grace.*

23. William Temple, Christian-quotes.ochristian.com/ William-Temple-Quotes/

# Chapter 6

24. Bennis and Nanus, *Leaders,* 96.

25. Bennis and Thomas, *Geeks and Geezers,* 123.

26. Browning, "Aurora Leigh," ll 61-64.

27. McKenna, *The Jesus Model,* 43.

28. Brown, *The Boys in the Boat.*

## Chapter 7

29. Margot Asquith, www.brainyquote.com/quotes/authors/m/
margot_asquith.html

## Chapter 8

30. Gaiman, *The Sandman: The Kindly Ones,* Book IX.

31. Hine, *"How Great Thou Art."*

## Chapter 9

32. Beattie, *More Language of Letting Go,* 15.

33. www.quoteinvestigator.com/2010/05/28/golf-good-walk/

34. Quoted in Sjogren, *Conspiracy of Kindness,* 120.

## Chapter 11

35. Roger A. Caras quotes, www.goodreads.com/author/
quotes/85216

36. Daniel H. Burham, Director of Works, World's Columbian
Exposition, 1893, quoted in front matter of Larson, *The Devil
in the White City.*

37. Schumacher, *Small Is Beautiful.* 505.

38. Peterson, "Slow Me Down, Lord," webtree.ca/inspiration/
slowmedown.html

39. Text by Katharina von Schlegal, trans. by Jane L. Borthwick
*"Be Still My Soul."*

## Chapter 12

40. M. Acklam, quotable.es/quotes/by/m-acklam

---

# Bibliography

Acklam, M. quotable.es/quotes/by/m-acklam

Asquith, Margot. www.brainyquote.com/quotes/authors/m/margot_asquith.html

Beattie, Melody. *More Language of Letting Go.* Center City, MN: Hazelden, 2000.

Bennis, Warren G. and Burt Nanus. *Leaders: Strategies for Taking Charge.* New York: Harper and Row, 1985.

———. and Robert Thomas. *Geeks and Geezers.* Boston: Harvard Business School Press, 2002.

Brown, Daniel James Brown. *The Boys In the Boat.* New York: Viking, 2013.

Browning, Elizabeth Barrett. *"Aurora Leigh."*

Caras, Roger A. www.goodreads.com/author/quotes/85216

Carney, Glandion with Marjean Brooks. *The Way of Grace: Finding God in the Path of Surrender.* Downers Grove, IL: IVP, 2014.

Gaiman, Neil. *The Sandman: The Kindly Ones,* Book IX. Los Angeles, CA: Vertigo, 2012.

Graham, Billy. www.brainyquotes.com/quotes/quotes/billygraham390334.html

Hine, Stuart K. (text and music). *"How Great Thou Art."*

Larson, Erik. *The Devil in the White City: Murder, Magic and Madness at the Fair that Changed the World.* New York: Crown, 2003.

Lewis, C. S. *The Problem of Pain.* An Amazon Company: CreateSpace Independent Publishers Platform, 2014.

McKenna, David L. *The Jesus Model.* Waco, Texas: Word, 1977.

———. *Retirement is Not for Sissies.* Newburgh, Oregon: Barclay, 2003.

Miller, Merle. *Plain Speaking: An Oral Biography of Harry S. Truman.* Berkeley, CA: Berkeley, 1974.

Paulon, Terry. *"A Call for Convicted Civility."* Townhall.com/ . . . /2013/06/17 a-call-for-convicted-civility-n1620233

Peterson, Wilfred Arlan. *"Slow Me Down, Lord."* webtree.ca/inspiration/slowmedown.html

Powell, Colin, quoted in Oren Harari. *A Leadership Primer.* govleaders.org/Powell.htm quoteinvestigator.com/2010/05/28/golf-good-walk/

Schultz, Charles. *Happiness is a Warm Puppy*. Kennebunkport, ME: Cedar Mill, 2006.

Schumacher, E. F. *Small Is Beautiful: A Study of Economics As If People Mattered*. New York: Harper and Row, 1973.

Sjogren, Steve. *Conspiracy of Kindness: A Refreshing New Approach to Sharing the Love of Jesus With Others*. Minneapolis, MN: Bethany House, 1993.

St. Francis. www.historyplace.com/speeches/st.fran.htm

Temple, William. Christian-quotes.ochristian.com/William-Temple-Quotes/

von Schlegal, Katharina (text), trans. Jane L. Borthwick. *"Be Still My Soul."*

Wesley, John. *"The General Deliverance,"* Sermon 60 (1782). Wesley.nnu.edu/ . . . /sermon-60 -the-general-deliverance/

Yancey, Philip. *Vanishing Grace: Whatever Happened to the Good News?* Grand Rapids, MI: Zondervan, 2014.